WATERSIDE
In Shropshire

Peter Kerr

COUNTRYSIDE BOOKS

NEWBURY, BERKSHIRE

COUNTRYSIDE BOOKS
3 Catherine Road
Newbury, Berkshire

ISBN 1 85306 615 X

To view our complete range of books,
please visit us at
www.countrysidebooks.co.uk

Designed by Graham Whiteman
Cover illustration by Colin Doggett
Maps and photographs by the author

Produced through MRM Associates Ltd., Reading
Typeset by Techniset Typesetters, Newton-le-Willows
Printed by J. W. Arrowsmith Ltd, Bristol

Contents

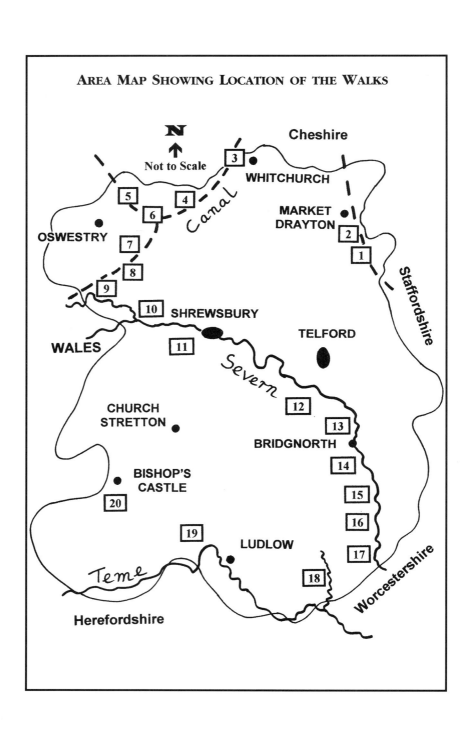

AREA MAP SHOWING LOCATION OF THE WALKS

N

Not to Scale

Cheshire

3

WHITCHURCH

5

4

Canal

6

MARKET
DRAYTON

OSWESTRY

7

2

1

8

Staffordshire

9

10

SHREWSBURY

WALES

11

TELFORD

Severn

12

CHURCH
STRETTON

13

BRIDGNORTH

14

BISHOP'S
CASTLE

15

20

16

19

17

LUDLOW

Teme

18

Worcestershire

Herefordshire

Walk

INTRODUCTION

The beautiful county of Shropshire, stretching from the Welsh border to the northern midlands, covers over 1,200 square miles and offers a diversity of scenery, from the 'blue remembered hills' in the south, alluded to by A.E. Housman in *A Shropshire Lad*, to the northern plain that merges with that of Cheshire. The county also has numerous rivers, from the mighty River Severn to the smaller Teme, Onny, Vyrnwy, Tern, Clun, Camlad, Perry, Corve, Rea and Kemp, all of which find their way directly, or indirectly, to the Severn. Add to this the fact that the county is part of the Welsh Border Country, the Marches, with a chequered history that includes border warfare, Roman occupation, Civil War campaigns, the birth of the Industrial Revolution at Ironbridge, and the canal age, then it all bodes well for locating interesting walks.

With so many rivers in the county the task of researching suitable 'Waterside Walks', to include beautiful scenery, historical interest, a good hostelry and to cover the whole of the county, did not seem problematical but, with the exception of the Severn, very few of the rivers have rights of way along them. However, by locating possible walks on the map, an interesting pattern emerged. Starting in the north east, near Market Drayton, the walks follow an 'S' shape across the county, using canals in the north (Shropshire Union, Llangollen and Montgomery), then rivers (Vyrnwy, Severn, Rea, Teme and Kemp), and some smaller brooks, to finish with the tip of the 'S' at Bishop's Castle. The walks have also been varied in length, from 2¹/₂ to 8¹/₂ miles, and cover a wide variety of walking surfaces, including canal towpaths, riverside paths, country roads and field paths. To give further flexibility, nine of the walks have an alternative length, and some can be joined to give even longer routes. The locations have been specifically chosen to visit interesting places such as Market Drayton, Whitchurch, Ellesmere, Ironbridge, Bridgnorth, Cleobury Mortimer, Ludlow and Bishop's Castle, and to follow the history of the canals and the River Severn. One thing every walk has is a good hostelry, all tried and tested, either on the walk or at the start (and finish). With the above combination, each walk is designed to give a full, and interesting, day out.

Shropshire, however, is not just about rivers and canals, as it has some 8,000 rights of way covering 3,000 miles. It also has a long distance footpath of its own, the Shropshire Way (see Walk 20) and a similar bridlepath, the Jack Mytton Way (see Walk 5). The new Severn Way (see Walks 12 – 17) also runs through the county and sections of all three have been included in the routes. All the walks in the book are on rights of way or permissive paths, such as canal towpaths, and were open and usable when the route was researched in the summer of 1999. However, problems can occur and if they do, can be referred to the appropriate authority – rights of way to Shropshire County Council, Shirehall, Abbey Foregate, Shrewsbury, and canal towpaths to British Waterways, Canal Offices, Birch, Ellesmere, Shropshire. Currently Ordnance Survey are phasing out the Pathfinder maps and replacing them with Explorer maps, so where the new Explorer map is known the information is included in the walk notes.

On a personal note, the writing of this book has been a journey of discovery and nostalgia. My main walking activities, and previous books, have been in Worcestershire and south Shropshire, so the area north of the River Severn was largely 'new' walking territory; it was a fantastic and enjoyable experience. On the nostalgia side my very first holiday was at a farm near Llangollen, and I can still recall fishing for 'tiddlers' in the Llangollen Canal near the Horseshoe Falls. Following the Llangollen and Montgomery Canal brought back boyhood memories, and the Shropshire Union Canal section recalled doing the Four Counties Ring about seven years ago. If readers only have a fraction of the enjoyment this book has given me in writing it, I am sure you will find its acquisition worthwhile.

Peter Kerr

CHESWARDINE AND THE SHROPSHIRE UNION CANAL

❦

In an unspoilt part of north-east Shropshire close to the Staffordshire border, this thoroughly enjoyable walk includes villages of quiet charm, field paths and a section of the Shropshire Union Canal, with sweeping views across Shropshire from the Wrekin northwards.

The Wharf Tavern at the side of the canal

The parish of Cheswardine is a quiet rural area on the county boundary with Staffordshire. Indeed, at the time of the Domesday Book, the entry recording the village placed it in Staffordshire. Also listed was a small castle, long since demolished. The nearest thing to a national highway hereabouts is probably the Shropshire Union Canal, which has had a complicated history and a number of name changes. The original scheme, for a more direct link between the rivers Mersey and Severn, only came to fruition when this section of the canal opened from Nantwich to Autherley Junction near

Wolverhampton, thus linking the then Ellesmere Canal to the Staffordshire and Worcestershire Canal. The previous route was the long haul through the Staffordshire Potteries via the Trent and Mersey Canal. One of the last canals to be completed (opened in 1835 as the Birmingham and Liverpool Junction Canal), the Shropshire Union (main branch) took the most direct route instead of following contour lines, and therefore has some high embankments and deep cuttings. Woodseaves Cutting, north of Cheswardine, at almost 100 feet deep is dark, damp and claustrophobic. The complete canal system, from Ellesmere Port on the Mersey down to near Wolverhampton, eventually became the Shropshire Union Canal, including the branches now referred to as the Llangollen and Montgomery canals.

Cheswardine village (two inns) and Soudley (one inn) are not on a main road, so retain their tranquillity, but this also means that the inns may not be open lunch times in midweek. However, along the canal there are places originally provided for loading/unloading, as well as places for turning the narrowboats, referred to as 'winding holes'. Both can be seen at Goldstone Wharf at Bridge 55. Here The Wharf Tavern, with a large canal-side garden, now caters for all refreshment requirements and is open seven days a week (food from 12 noon to 2 pm and 7 pm to 9.30 pm). This very popular hostelry offers a range of beers, wines and food, specialising in meat and fish grills, and also has daily specials. My own personal choice was a large T bone steak (yes, a real one!) and chunky chips (and salad!). Telephone: 01630 661226.

- **HOW TO GET THERE:** Cheswardine is situated about 4 miles southeast of Market Drayton. It is signposted from the A529.
- **PARKING:** In Lawn Lane at the side of the church or in the High Street. No parking restrictions.
- **LENGTH OF THE WALK:** 3½ or 4½ miles. Map: OS Explorer 243 Market Drayton (GR 719299).

THE WALK

1. The walk starts by the church, St Swithun's, which has 13th century origins but is mainly of 19th century reconstruction. Take the lane opposite The Fox and Hounds, signposted Chipnall and Doley. Go along the road for about 350 yards, cross a stile on the right, and then go over the field to an iron kissing gate. Continue

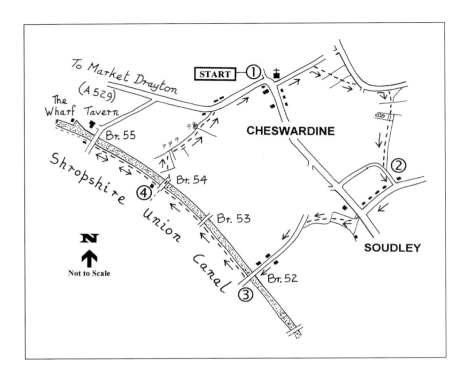

ahead to another stile, then over a field to a stile by a large oak tree. Turn right along the road, following it as it sweeps left (ignore the small lane going right). Some 250 yards beyond the bend cross a stile on the right (careful, shallow ditch in front), then cross the edge of the field to a stile by two large gates. Now bear slightly right, crossing the open field to a footbridge. Once over follow the left hedge to a gate to a lane and turn left.

2. Go along the lane to a road junction and turn right. Note the old ornate iron signpost. Continue along the road (now in Soudley), past houses and farm buildings on the right, and at a road junction cross to a field gate opposite. The Wheatsheaf Inn is 50 yards to the right. Once through the gate, with a view of the Wrekin directly ahead, go part right to a hedge corner. This is a meadow so the long grass can be quite wet after rain, as I soon discovered! On reaching the hedge corner again go part right, across the field, towards a group of trees at what is now the far left corner. Cross a stile about 40 yards to the right of the corner, then follow the left edge of the field as it sweeps right to join a road. Turn left and follow the road to the canal bridge at Little Soudley.

3. Cross the canal bridge (Bridge 52), then join the towpath via a gate on the left. Go under the bridge going northward along the towpath of the Shropshire Union Canal, enjoying the view, left, over the North Shropshire Plain towards the Wrekin. The narrowboats using the canal now are pleasure boats for holidays, but for over 100 years this canal was used for commercial traffic until its final demise in the 1950s. Continue under two more bridges (note the iron bollards to protect the bridge masonry from the tow ropes, and the resulting grooves), to a point some 20 yards past the second bridge, by a small brick building. This is Point 4. Walkers wishing to do the short walk only go to '4' below, those wishing to visit The Wharf Tavern, or just enjoy the full walk, proceed to the next bridge (No. 55) to see the narrowboat moorings, the winding hole, and the 'stop planks' in the small brick hut. At various points along a canal, usually at bridges, vertical grooves can be seen down either side of the canal. In the event of repairs being required, the planks are placed across the canal using the grooves, and the isolated section can then be drained. Then go over the bridge to the inn. After refreshments retrace your steps to Point 4. Notice the canal milepost some 100 yards south of the bridge.

4. To return to Cheswardine, take the path going away from the towpath near the brick building, sweeping left to a track and then over the bridge. Now go part left to a gate in the hedge, then proceed to a stile in the far right field corner. Cross two stiles close together, then follow the left hedge, over two more stiles, to reach the road (by some houses). Turn right and follow the road back to Cheswardine.

PLACES OF INTEREST NEARBY
Hodnet Hall Gardens, some 7 miles west of Cheswardine, on the A53 at Hodnet, are 60 acres of flowers, trees, sweeping lawns and ornamental pools. Open from 12 noon to 5 pm on Tuesday to Sunday and Bank Holiday Mondays, between April and September. Telephone: 01630 685202.

THE SHROPSHIRE UNION CANAL
AND MARKET DRAYTON

This is a walk of contrasts that takes in an old market town, the River Tern, country lanes, and the Shropshire Union Canal (including the five locks at Tyrley)

The marina at Market Drayton

The small town of Market Drayton, in existence at the time of the Domesday Book, was granted its market in 1245. It still has a thriving street market every Wednesday, when the town centre is crowded and parking difficult. The town's other claims to fame are that Robert Clive (of India) was born nearby in 1725, and that it is the home of gingerbread, which has been baked in the town for over 200 years.

To the east runs the Shropshire Union Canal, which brought trade to the town in the 19th century, being a link between the River Mersey, Birmingham and the River Severn. When the canals were first built their main cargoes consisted of heavy goods, difficult to transport by road, such as coal and limestone. Subsequently on this section of the canal agricultural goods predominated, including fruit, Cheshire cheese and milk. Here at Market Drayton the canal system now has a boatyard, a marina and narrowboat moorings for visiting the town for refreshment. (Much needed when going south, after negotiating the 15 locks at Audlem and the five at Adderley, as the author once did).

There are numerous hostelries in Market Drayton, but the eating place chosen for this walk is The Four Alls Inn, as it is near the half way point. It is also open seven days a week, (food available from 12 noon to 2 pm and 6 pm to 9 pm). There is a range of 'lunchtime specials', and it is well known for the excellent three course 'Senior Citizens' lunch which ensures that it has a regular clientele (I was tempted to lie about my age!). My own choice was local sausage with onion gravy (very tasty), with vegetables served separately on a side dish. The main beer is Whitbread's and there are always guest beers. Telephone: 01630 652995.

- **HOW TO GET THERE:** The town is at the junction of the A53 and the A529.
- **PARKING:** At the free public car park near to the Market Drayton Swimming Centre and adjacent picnic area, off the A529 just south of the town centre.
- **LENGTH OF THE WALK:** 4 miles (up to 5 miles with the optional extensions). Map: OS Explorer 243 Market Drayton (GR 676339).

THE WALK

1. Return to the entrance to the car park on the A529, Newport Road. Turn left and then left again into Newtown, now walking along a small channel of the River Tern (the main channel is by the picnic area). Continue past the Swimming Centre in Walkmill Road, passing houses on the right, to reach a junction of several roads. Here turn left, signposted Market Drayton Golf Club.

2. Follow this road for about 250 yards from the road junction, twice crossing bridges over channels of the River Tern. Now turn left into Sandy Lane, continuing along this unmade lane for well over $1/2$ mile (the reason for the name of the lane soon becoming apparent). To the right is the golf course and on the left are paddocks and isolated

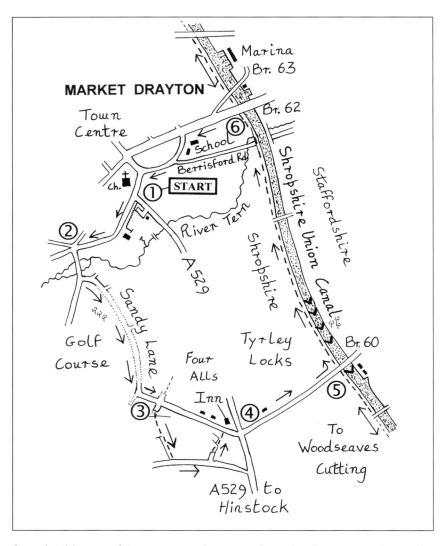

MARKET DRAYTON

Town Centre

Marina
Br. 63

Br. 62

School

Berrisford Rd

Ch. †

① START

River Tern

⑥

Staffordshire

Shropshire Union Canal

Shropshire

A 529

② ←

Golf Course

Sandy Lane

Four Alls Inn

Tyrley Locks

Br. 60

③

④

⑤

To Woodseaves Cutting

A529 to Hinstock

farm buildings; of interest are the animal tracks that come down the banks and cross the lane. As the lane becomes a tarmac surface and sweeps left, follow it, ignoring the unmade track going ahead. Then, some 200 yards from the bend look for an enclosed track on the right. Now it is decision time. Ramblers who enjoy walking on tarmac roads, continue to follow the lane to The Four Alls Inn (Point 4). Those wanting a more 'stileish' walk continue as below.

3. Take the enclosed track going right, off the road. It may possibly be wet and muddy after rain. Soon cross a stile by a gate, then continue across the open field aiming for a small group of trees. Join a hedge (on right) and on reaching a lane turn left. Some 200 yards along the lane turn left onto another track and proceed to, and go through, an old gate. Now follow the right hedge for about 50 yards, cross a stile and follow the left hedge. As the hedge turns sharp left keep the same direction as before, aiming for the left end of The Four Alls Inn, to reach a stile to the road opposite the inn. (Good that, wasn't it? Also, those walkers who took the short route will have a drink waiting for you!)

4. On leaving The Four Alls Inn take time to look at the sign – does the last one sound familiar? 'I Rule All. I Fight for All. I Pray for All. But, I Pay for All.' Cross the A529, take the road opposite Sandy Lane and reach the Tyrley Locks, with the wharf, cottages (dated 1837) and the narrowboat turning point, called a 'winding hole'. Join the towpath of the Shropshire Union Canal via the gate on the right, before crossing the bridge, then go left and under the bridge (Bridge 60). At this point it is possible, before continuing with the walk, to make a short detour to the start of the Woodseaves Cutting. To do this do not go under Bridge 60 but walk south, along the canal towpath, to pass under Bridge 59. A little further on you enter the cutting, but be warned, it can be dark and wet, and there are towpath erosion problems. When ready return to Bridge 60 to continue the walk.

5. At Tyrley there are five locks, out of only seven on the section of canal between Market Drayton and Autherley Junction near Wolverhampton. Now you can watch people working the locks while you enjoy a leisurely stroll along the canal towpath, which is also the Shropshire/Staffordshire border at this point, the canal being in Staffordshire (so don't fall in!). On reaching Tyrley Bottom Lock the canal has already entered the Tyrley Cutting, the canal being cut by hand through a sandstone outcrop. On leaving the cutting proceed under Bridge 61 and enjoy the view, left, towards Market Drayton, with the church tower dominating the skyline. Soon the canal crosses high over the Tern valley, being elevated on an embankment, then over an aqueduct above Berrisford Road (a route into the town). Now continue past the boat moorings to reach

Tyrley Top Lock

Bridge 62, Newcastle Road, the route back to the start. Before returning to the start, if time permits, go under the bridge and onto, and beyond, Bridge 63 to view the boatyard, the water supply point, more boat moorings and the marina, a hive of activity in the holiday season.

6. To return to the start go up to the road at Bridge 62 and turn left, following the signs to the town centre if you want to visit the shops, etc, and from there to the Swimming Centre. Or take the direct route back by turning left into Great Hales Road, just past the school, then left again at Phoenix Bank and thus reach Newport Road and the car park.

PLACES OF INTEREST NEARBY

Hawkstone Park is situated at Weston under Redcastle, off the A422, 7 miles south-west of Market Drayton. Created in the 18th century, the park has a series of pathways, grottoes and follies. It is open daily from April to October and at weekends from January to March. Telephone: 01939 200611.

WALK 3

WHITCHURCH AND GRINDLEY BROOK LOCKS

An interesting and varied walk that includes the oldest inhabited town in Shropshire, field paths, and the Llangollen Canal. The canal section passes the spectacular 'staircase locks' at Grindley Brook.

The canal seen from Bridge 26

Whitchurch was founded by the Romans in AD 70 as a camp part way between Wroxeter and Chester. The Saxons also settled here, the Lord of the Manor being Earl (later King) Harold (he of eye and arrow fame). When the Saxon church of St Alkmund was replaced by a Norman one a white stone was used, resulting in the town being called 'Whitechurch', now Whitchurch. During the 19th century the canal brought considerable prosperity to Whitchurch, with a canal arm extending to a wharf and warehousing in the town centre but, with rail travel being faster, and roads improving, it fell into disuse and only a short section is still intact. However, plans are

17

well advanced to reopen part of the abandoned canal to create mooring facilities close to the town centre. Today, the Llangollen Canal is a 46 mile waterway that follows the land contours through a variety of scenery. An unusual canal feature is that it has continual running water, being used to convey water for other canal systems (approx. 8 million gallons per day) from the River Dee to Hurleston Reservoir at the junction with the main branch of the Shropshire Union Canal. The flow of water is particularly apparent at locks, so this walk has been routed to include the Grindley Brook Locks, six locks in two sets of three, one set being 'staircase' locks.

At about the mid point on the walk, The Horse and Jockey is situated on the A41 at Grindley Brook. First recorded as an inn about 1780 (although parts of the building are older), it was extended in 1953 and now caters for boaters from the canal, ramblers and holidaymakers. The menu is aimed at people out for the day and is based on good wholesome food at reasonable prices. Their speciality dish (the author's choice at the time) is steak and kidney pie, prepared on the premises and served in individual square dishes with a pastry topping. The main beer is Banks and there is always a guest beer. Food is served from 12 noon to 2 pm and 7 pm to 9 pm, all week. Telephone: 01948 662723.

- **HOW TO GET THERE:** The town is situated south-east of the junction of the A41 and the A49 (which form the town bypass). Follow the signs to the town centre.
- **PARKING:** There are a number of free long stay car parks in the town, the largest being by the swimming baths and the Tesco supermarket. Do ensure that a 'long stay' car park is used.
- **LENGTH OF THE WALK:** 5 miles. Map: OS Explorer 257 Crewe and Nantwich (GR 542416).

THE WALK

1. Start the walk from the Civic Centre in High Street, going northwards and past St Alkmund's church and along Bargates (the church is usually open). Continue straight ahead at the first roundabout and then take the right fork at the second roundabout (Tarporley Road). Follow this road for some 600 yards and turn left onto a gravel lane, hidden until reached. Follow the lane, ignoring a track to the left, for about 300 yards then cross a stile to the right of a gateway.

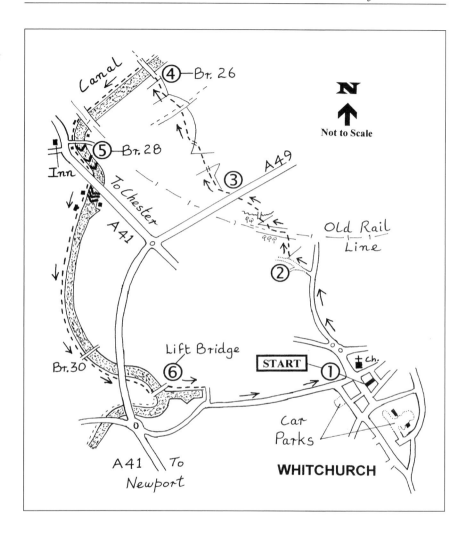

2. Go across the open field on the well used path to another stile, then turn left immediately past the trees. The route now follows a disused railway track of the old London and North Western Railway for over 200 yards, then crosses a stile in the fence over to the right. (In summer the stile may be hidden by undergrowth so be careful not to continue too far along the old railway line.) This is an official footpath diversion that may not be shown on some older OS maps.

Once over turn left and soon cross a stile and footbridge (crossing the second stile is optional!). Initially follow the left tree line and stream, and then cross the end of a field to a stile in the far hedge (careful, ditch beyond). Cross the A49 to another ditch crossing and stile opposite.

3. Now go part left, across the field, to a stile by an electricity pole, then turn and initially follow the right hedge line. Cross the corner of the field to a stile and deep ditch crossing at a hedge. Go straight across the field (keeping right of an electricity pole) to a stile in a fence. Keep the same direction, across the field corner, to another ditch crossing and stile. In the next field go part right over the large open field to cross a stile by an electricity pole, at the very far corner and not visible until part way over the field. Now go across the field ahead to cross another stile in a fence and then follow the right fence, over yet another stile (the last on this walk) to reach Bridge 26 over the Llangollen Canal.

4. Cross the bridge (into Cheshire), turning right to join the towpath, then go under the bridge and follow the canal. At this point the canal is the boundary between Cheshire and Shropshire, and this section of towpath is part of the Sandstone Trail, a 30 mile path between Grindley Brook and Frodsham; a signboard at The Horse and Jockey gives further information. Follow the towpath to pass through a small tunnel (actually the bridge over the canal for the disused railway line), now re-entering Shropshire. At the next bridge (No 28), the lane to the right leads to the A41 and The Horse and Jockey Inn, a very welcome stop after all those stiles!

5. From The Horse and Jockey Inn return to Bridge 28, to continue along the canal towpath. Pass the first three of the Grindley Brook locks, noting the continual flow of water around the locks, go under the A41, and immediately encounter the three 'staircase' locks. This is a set of three locks together where the top gate of one lock is the bottom gate of the next. The operation of these locks is interesting to watch, particularly when boats are going down and the locks are already full, this causes the next lock down to overflow in quite a spectacular fashion. Pass the Lockside Stores (ice cream and other goodies!), and the old Lock Keepers Cottage and notice the 'winding hole' (a narrow boat turning point) on the opposite side of the

A Dutch-style lift bridge

canal. Continue on the towpath, past the boat mooring area and then under bridges 30 and 30A (the A41 again) to reach the New Mills Lift Bridge, a Dutch-stile canal bridge. This type of bridge was sometimes installed as it was less costly than a stone bridge. Cross over this to join the Whitchurch Arm of the canal.

6. Follow the towpath to the end of the canal arm, and note the 'winding hole' on the opposite bank to enable the narrow boats to turn around. Go up the steps and then over the bridge. At the main road turn left and follow it (Smallbrook Road, Sherrymill Hill and Yardington) back to St Alkmund's church and the Civic Centre.

PLACES OF INTEREST NEARBY
Some 2 miles south of the town, just off the A41, is the *Brown Moss Nature Reserve*, with parking and Nature Trails, consisting of small meres, peat bog, heath and woodland. A place to just sit and relax or to explore. An unusual feature of Brown Moss is the varying water level, so sometimes the Nature Trails can be under water! It is also a Site of Special Scientific Interest (SSSI).

THE SHROPSHIRE LAKE DISTRICT

୶ୖୖୖ୶

This is just too good to miss, an easy longer walk that visits three meres and includes a 3 mile towpath section, with constantly changing views and time to contemplate the results of glacial action thousands of years ago.

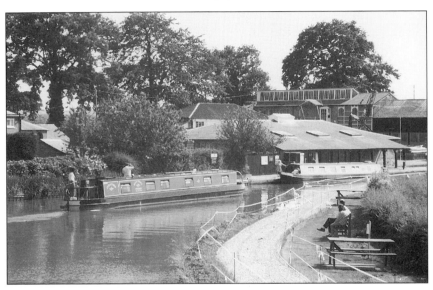

The Llangollen Canal

Ellesmere, an old market town that goes back to Saxon times, is situated in what is known as the Shropshire Lake District, with the meres, six in number, to the east of the town. They came into existence at the time of the last Ice Age, when retreating glaciers scoured out the land to leave hollows which filled from the melting ice. The 19th century saw a surge of prosperity at Ellesmere with the construction of the canal, the town canal arm testifying to the trade that took place. The section of the Llangollen Canal included in this walk is pleasant and tranquil and, because it follows the contour lines, meanders through the countryside with continual changing views.

The Sun Inn at Welshampton has a reputation for enjoyable food and is popular with both visitors and local people. Food is available from 12 noon to 2 pm Tuesday to Sunday, and 7 pm to 9 pm all week. The full menu offers meat and fish grills, vegetarian dishes, a range of snacks, daily specials (my own choice being pork chops, two large ones), pensioners' specials and a children's menu. The beer range is Greenalls and Tetley. Telephone: 01948 710637.

- **HOW TO GET THERE:** Ellesmere is situated at the junction of the A495 and the A528.
- **PARKING:** Free parking is available in the car parks at, or near, the town centre (the start of the walk). The car parks at The Mere (other than roadside parking) are 'Pay and Display'.
- **LENGTH OF THE WALK:** 7 or 8½ miles. Map: OS Explorer 241 Shrewsbury (GR 401349).

THE WALK

1. Leave the town centre car park at the Watergate Street exit, by The Ellesmere inn, turn left and follow the street to the main road (Church Street). Turn right along the road, crossing over when convenient and passing the parish church of the Blessed Virgin Mary on the right, to reach The Mere. This is the largest of the six meres, covering 116 acres and over 60 feet deep. The route now enters Cremorne Gardens and follows the well defined path that keeps close to the lake shore. Continue around the mere to the north shore, through woodland and patches of giant rhododendrons, and enjoy spotting the wild life, squirrels, birds, dragonflies, etc. Cross a stile into more open ground, then another back into woodland, then a third into an open meadow. Here turn left, signposted Welshampton.

2. Follow the left fence/hedge to cross a stile, (boggy ground to the right). Continue along the left side of an arable field to another stile, located immediately past some trees. Here, first go left, then head towards the farm buildings, passing through a gate, to reach a stile in the far corner of the next field. Now go ahead, staying on a wide meandering track that ends at a field. Go straight up the slope to a stile, visible when near the top, then straight across an arable field (aim for the right end of the near tree line ahead). Cross a stile to a very wide track and turn right.

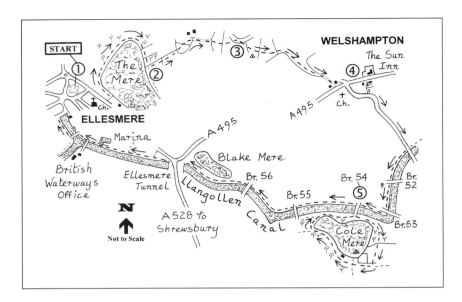

3. Keep on the wide track for almost 100 yards, cross a stile on the right. Cross the corner of the field to another stile and go straight ahead over an open field. Note the old OS Triangulation Point over to the right; these are now redundant as the OS maps are produced by aerial survey. Once over the brow of the field go to a stile, visible in the fence ahead. Now proceed over a large arable field, the destination being the very far corner. This is not visible from the stile, so if the route is not apparent aim for an isolated tree at the top of the field. On reaching the field corner use the gate (or stile), following the right hedge as it turns right and leads into an enclosed track. Follow the track, through a farmyard, to the A495. Turn left and proceed to The Sun Inn.

4. Now being suitably refreshed, take the footpath opposite the inn car park, passing shops on the right and then a house garage on the left. Keep on the enclosed track (little choice really!), join a lane and turn left, following it for just over ½ mile to reach the Llangollen Canal. Go down the steps on the left of the bridge to join the towpath, then under the bridge. Now relax and enjoy a 3 mile towpath walk with no navigation worries. Follow the towpath under Bridge 52, past Lyneal Wharf at Bridge 53 then stop and make a decision at Bridge 54, Point 5. This is named Yell Bridge on OS maps but Miss Each Bridge on the canal map, so take your pick! Anyone wishing to do an extra 1¹/₂ miles around Cole Mere (which is visible from the towpath) read on; those wishing to go directly back to Ellesmere see '5' below.

THE COLE MERE EXTENSION: Cole Mere is part of the Cole Mere Country Park, administered by Shropshire County Council, and is used for fishing and yachting as well as supporting an abundance of wildlife. To walk around Cole Mere take the steps on the right before going under Bridge 54. Cross the bridge and turn left, following the well defined path, first alongside the canal, then downhill and meandering through woodland (ignore side paths) to reach a gate. Go straight across the field to another gate, turn right and follow the fence of the yacht enclosure. At a path junction keep ahead, now on a right of way, pass the club house, and continue alongside Cole Mere. On approaching the end of the mere look for a path going off to the right. After about 20 yards go through a gate, now back on a permissive path, then use another gate and a footbridge, and at a path junction turn right. Continue on this prominent path which first keeps near the mere shore, then gradually moves away from it, finally going uphill to Bridge 54. Rejoin the towpath and continue as below.

5. Continuing under Bridge 54, pass under Bridge 55, then past a 'winding hole' (a boat turning point on the opposite bank). Pass Bridge 56 and also the attractive and quiet Blake Mere (time to pause and watch the herons). On reaching the Ellesmere Tunnel (approx. 100 yards) either go through, but be warned it is dark and wet in places, or go up the steps, cross the A528 and rejoin the towpath at the other side. Proceed past the Blackwater Meadow Marina to reach the footbridge over the Ellesmere Arm of the Llangollen Canal. Cross the bridge and turn right. Follow the Ellesmere Arm to the end. Turn right into Wharf Road, passing the old wharf crane, then right again at the top to regain the town centre.

PLACES OF INTEREST NEARBY

Ellesmere and the meres are in themselves one of the tourist attractions of north Shropshire, having a Visitor Centre, a Country Park, parks, gardens, an Arboretum, abundant wildlife, an attractive church and an old castle site. Full details from the Visitor and Tourist Information Centre at The Mere. Telephone 01691 622981.

HINDFORD ON THE LLANGOLLEN CANAL

Away from any towns, yet full of interest, this level walk has sweeping views towards the hills on the English/Welsh border.

The canal near the Jack Mytton Inn

Hindford is a small hamlet situated to the north-east of Whittington, consisting of farms, houses and the Jack Mytton Inn. 'Mad Jack' Mytton (1796–1834) was a local squire who lived at Halston Hall, about 1 mile south of Hindford. A one time MP for Shrewsbury, he was known as a great sportsman, particularly in horsemanship, and apparently enjoyed large quantities of ale and wine. For ramblers there is a lasting legacy in the Jack Mytton Way, a 70 mile long bridleway through south Shropshire between Highley and Llanfair Waterdine. The 2 mile section of the Llangollen Canal included in this walk is relatively straight, with sweeping views west towards Oswestry and Llanymynech, and south towards the Breiddens.

The Jack Mytton Inn (known locally as Mad Jack's) is a canal-side hostelry with a large garden that caters for locals, visitors and boaters, and can be particularly busy at weekends. The inn has an extensive menu ranging from curry to grills as well as sandwiches and baked potatoes, with daily specials that include such dishes as braised pheasant, local wild rabbit and swordfish steak (my choice, as the owner assured me it had been caught in the canal that morning!). The beer range includes Minsterley Premium Ale, Old Speckled Hen and Timothy Taylor 'Landlord'. It is open every day with food served from 12 noon to 2.30 pm and 7 pm to 9 pm. Telephone: 01691 679861.

- **HOW TO GET THERE:** Hindford is located less than 1 mile north of the A495 Whittington to Ellesmere road, the turn off signposted about 1 mile east of Whittington.
- **PARKING:** At a small parking area in the lane outside the Jack Mytton Inn, or in the wide section of road through the hamlet. Patrons of the Jack Mytton Inn can use their car park but please contact the owner first (telephone: 01691 679861).
- **LENGTH OF THE WALK:** 3 or 5 miles. It can be linked with Walk 6 to become up to 11½ miles. Map: OS Explorer 240 Oswestry (GR 335330).

THE WALK

1. From the entrance to The Jack Mytton Inn car park go to the T junction in Hindford and turn right. Follow the road for about 600 yards. The Welsh border and the Offa's Dyke Path run along the raised ground on the horizon. On reaching a road junction cross the stile on the right, by a gate, and cross the field to a gateway and stile in the opposite hedge. When I walked this way a field over to the left was full of bright red poppies. In the next field go diagonally across to a stile in the far left corner (careful, big step down), then go part left to another stile in a fence. Now go part right, up and across a large open field (no aiming point) to the far corner. A stile should become visible from halfway across the field. Once over the stile cross the field towards a house to reach a stile and gate to a lane.

2. In the lane turn left and almost immediately left again at a junction. The border hills are now ahead again. At the next road

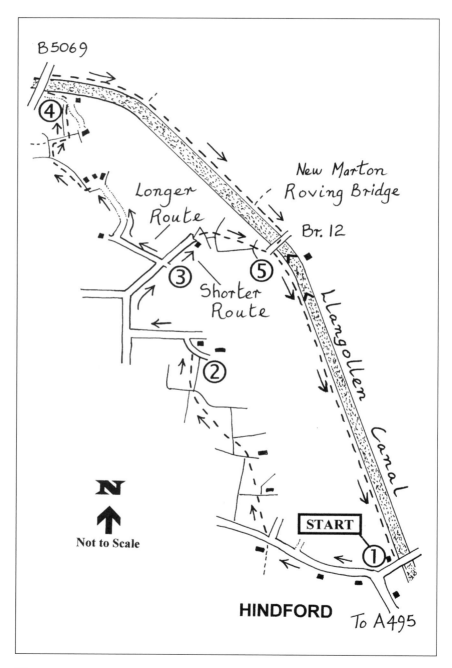

B5069

New Marton
Roving Bridge

Br. 12

Longer
Route

Llangollen Canal

③

Shorter
Route

⑤

④

②

N

Not to Scale

START

①

HINDFORD   To A495

The Llangollen Canal near Hindford

junction turn right, follow the road for some 500 yards and take the right fork. Then follow this road to where it sweeps left, a narrower lane going ahead, this is Point 3. Those ramblers doing the shorter walk read on, those doing the longer walk see '3' below.

SHORTER ROUTE: At the road junction keep ahead on the narrower road that soon becomes a stony track. At the end go through the gate ahead, alongside a house, then cross the house lawn to a stile to a field. On old maps the field came up to the house. Go over the corner of the field to a stile by a gate, then maintain the same direction over pasture land (narrow boats may now be visible ahead) to reach an overgrown stile and gate to the Llangollen Canal. This is Point 5, the route back being directly ahead on the canal towpath, the canal on the left.

3. For the longer route, follow the more prominent road as it sweeps left then, with a house drive ahead, goes right, becoming a stony track. Keep on the track as it turns left and heads towards a farm. The church tower visible over to the right is in the village of St Martin's. Immediately on entering a farmyard area look for a stile in the hedge over to the left (could be overgrown). Cross this, turn right and follow the right hedge, passing some farm buildings, for about 400 yards. Cross a stile on the right, follow the left field edge to the bottom corner and turn right (ignore the stile going left as that path can be very overgrown). Continue along the bottom of the field for some 60 yards then cross a stile on the left between two gates. Again follow the left hedge, join a house drive, then turn left at a lane and follow it to the B5069.

4. Turn right at the main road, cross the bridge over the canal and join the canal towpath heading back towards Hindford (canal on your right). Now it is a leisurely stroll along the wide towpath, with time to take in the views and exchange greetings with the boating fraternity. After about 1 mile reach Bridge 12, New Marton Roving Bridge. Cross it and turn left, the canal now on the left.

5. By taking a close look at the bridge you can see how, in a bygone age, a horse pulling a barge travelling towards Hindford could go over the bridge, then turn right and go under the bridge, thus avoiding the need to unhitch the tow rope. The reverse applied to horses going in the opposite direction. Now continue along the canal passing both the New Marton Top and Bottom Locks. Here it is worth noticing the side weirs prior to each lock. The Llangollen Canal is also a water channel so there is usually a continual flow of water even when the locks are not in use. Beyond New Marton Bottom Lock the towpath is uneven so please exercise care to avoid a dip in the canal. After a further mile of towpath the boat moorings at the Jack Mytton Inn are reached and some well earned refreshment is available.

PLACES OF INTEREST NEARBY

Some 4 miles north-west of Hindford is the imposing 700 year old *Chirk Castle*. Opening times and dates may vary slightly from year to year but generally it is open to the public 12 noon to 5 pm from April to September, all week except Monday and Tuesday (open Bank Holidays), and also at weekends only in October. Telephone: 01691 777701.

WELSH FRANKTON AND THE FRANKTON LOCKS

This walk is an interesting mixture of rural roads which give constantly changing views over north Shropshire towards the Welsh border, and a canal section that includes the Frankton Locks.

Bridge 1 on the canal

Welsh Frankton is a hamlet situated on the busy A495. The roads to the north, however, are quiet country lanes and, because of being slightly elevated, give sweeping views across the north Shropshire plain. Just south of Welsh Frankton is Lower Frankton, a quiet place now but once a very busy junction on this canal system.

What is now referred to as the Montgomery Canal started life as the Llanymynech Branch of the then Ellesmere Canal, completed in 1796 to access the vast limestone deposits being quarried at Llanymynech.

On this walk there is a choice of two inns for refreshment, the

Jack Mytton Inn at Hindford (see Walk 5) and the Narrow Boat Inn adjoining the A495. The Narrow Boat Inn lives up to its name, being long and narrow inside, but still having an extensive dining area. There are also benches to sit outside by the canal. Whilst the range of food is not as great as the Jack Mytton Inn, there is still ample choice to sustain the hungry rambler. Food is served every day between 12 noon to 2.30 pm and also 6 pm to 9 pm. Being a 'free house' there are always two guest beers as well as a range of lager, cider and wine. Telephone: 01691 661051.

- **HOW TO GET THERE:** Hindford is located less than 1 mile north of the A495 Whittington to Ellesmere road, the turn off signposted about 1 mile east of Whittington.
- **PARKING:** At a small parking area in the lane outside the Jack Mytton Inn, or in the wide section of road through the hamlet. Patrons of the Jack Mytton Inn can use their car park but please contact the owner first. Telephone: 01691 679861.
- **LENGTH OF THE WALK:** $2^1/_2$ or $6^1/_2$ miles. Can be increased to $11^1/_2$ miles by combining with Walk 5. Map: OS Explorer 240 Oswestry (GR 335330).

THE WALK

1. From the car park of the Jack Mytton Inn turn left, go over the canal bridge (Llangollen Canal) and follow the lane. At a road junction go right, signposted Lower Ridge and Perthy, and continue along this narrower lane as it sweeps right over a disused Cambrian Railway line. The lane now goes due south with a view ahead, weather permitting, towards Breidden Hill and Long Mountain in the far distance. Soon the lane sweeps left, passes a farm on the left, then meanders through the countryside. Some 500 yards past the farm look for a stile on the right, just prior to a sharp left hand bend. This is Point 2 on the map. For the shorter walk see immediately below, for the longer walk read on from '2'.

SHORTER ROUTE: Cross the stile on the right, turn left and follow the left hedge/fence. Then reach, after crossing a wire fence, the bridge over the canal. Cross the bridge (Point 6), going under it and following the tow path. Now see the notes from '6', below. (It is also possible to visit the Narrow Boat Inn by turning left, onto the canal towpath, before crossing the bridge, then returning to Point 6 to continue the walk.)

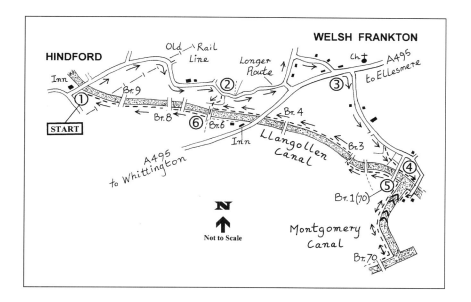

2. For the longer walk continue along the lane to a junction and turn left (this avoids the busy A495). After a further 400 yards take a narrow lane on the right and proceed into Welsh Frankton, taking time to enjoy the views over north-west Shropshire towards Wales.

3. Turn left along the A495, crossing as appropriate, then turn right at the next side road (to Lower Frankton) just before reaching the church. Follow this lane as it goes gently downhill, passing houses, a farm (Frankton Hall), and eventually sweeps right to a canal bridge. Do not cross the bridge but turn left to join the towpath. [For those of you who feel deprived of a field path, look for a stile on the right some 200 yards after passing a small track on the right (see map). Cross the stile, turn part left and follow the right hedge/fence line, open after the first section. Proceed ahead to cross two stiles, close together, in the far hedge, then follow the left hedge to a stile (or gate) to a lane (please be careful of the ditch just over the stile). Then turn right to the bridge.

4. Now for a tour of two canal junctions. This apparently remote junction was once a key point in the then Ellesmere Canal system. Hence the bridge numbers continued along the Montgomery canal and started from 1 again on the Llangollen Canal! Follow the towpath to the next bridge, No 69, passing a signpost listing the ends of the two canals, cross and follow the path around to the Montgomery Canal. Cross over the footbridge on the first two 'staircase' locks and follow the towpath (canal on the left) for about ½ mile. The route now passes two more of the Frankton locks and proceeds down to the real Bridge 70, Lockgate Bridge. The small canal arm here was to be the link to Shrewsbury, but the project was abandoned. Lockgate Bridge is a steep 'hump back' bridge and it is worth going to the top to see the scars left by unsuspecting motorists. When ready retrace your steps (canal on the right), noticing the canal mile post near the staircase lock, and follow the towpath around to Bridge No 1 (marked as No 70 as a result of an abandoned scheme of re-numbering) on the Llangollen Canal.

5. The walk continues along the towpath going under Bridge 1, a 'roving' or 'turnover' bridge. Pass under Bridge 2 then over Bridge 3, yet another 'roving' bridge, the canal now on the left. Please exercise care here as the canal bank has been eroded and may be narrow due to hedge growth. Continue under Bridge 4 to reach Bridge 5, the location of the Narrow Boat Inn. (If visiting the inn go over Bridge 5, the A495, then return to the towpath when fully replenished.) Continue past the marina and chandlers to reach Bridge 6, the joining point with the shorter walk. Cross this and continue along the canal, which is now on your right.

6. Bridge 6 is a classic example of a 'roving' bridge, where you can see from your own movements how a horse could cross over the canal without the need to unhitch the tow rope. Continue along the canal passing under bridges 7, 8 and 9, where old marks from the tow ropes are still faintly visible. Continue to the next bridge and the boat moorings at the Jack Mytton Inn.

PLACES OF INTEREST NEARBY
Only about 3 miles south-west of Hindford is *Oswestry*, an old border and market town with a number of attractions for visitors. There is a Tourist Information Centre at the Heritage Centre, located by the church (telephone: 01691 662753).

WALK 7

THE MONTGOMERY CANAL FROM QUEEN'S HEAD

They say good things come in small parcels and this short walk is no exception, a highly interesting ramble along the newly restored Montgomery Canal.

The Queen's Head inn

Well, which came first, Queen's Head or The Queen's Head? According to the inn it was The Queen's Head. This is the location where the then Llanymynech Branch of the Ellesmere Canal went under the then main road from London to Holyhead, so an inn was built to serve the needs of thirsty and hungry travellers. It was also the ideal place for a wharf, to bring in goods for local distribution and take out farm produce, and nearby was a flour mill and a sand pit, thus the village of Queen's Head came into existence.

Just over 1 mile north-east of Queen's Head is a short canal arm leading to a canal basin, here there were railway sidings and goods could be interchanged between rail and canal. Close by, on the opposite bank of the canal, is Rednal Wharf, a terminus for passengers who travelled by canal boat to join the train.

The Queen's Head is an inn that once served travellers from the canal and the A5. With the re-routing of the A5 it now attracts custom by the quality of the venue and by the quality and extent of the food offered. The menu gives a very large choice and covers four blackboards, ranging from meat or fish grills, fowl and game, snacks, pizzas, etc. All this good food can be washed down with some Theakston's beer or, if preferred, cider, lager, or a selection from the wine list. Food is served from 12 noon to 2.30 pm and 6 pm to 10 pm, all week. Telephone: 01691 610255.

- **HOW TO GET THERE:** Queen's Head is situated just off the A5 (junction with the B5009), some 4 miles south-east of Oswestry.
- **PARKING:** Car park by the canal opposite The Queen's Head.
- **LENGTH OF THE WALK:** 3 miles. It can be joined with Walk 8 to make a 9 mile walk. Map: OS Explorer 240 Oswestry (GR 339268).

THE WALK
Note: It is advisable not to do this walk in conditions of poor visibility, as at one point a main railway line must be crossed.

1. Leave the car park, turn left along the road then soon branch right along the B5009, signposted Whittington. (Care needed as there is no pedestrian sidewalk on this road.) After about 100 yards reach a stile on the right. The path from here soon crosses an arable field, and a compass or OS map might be required. If there is a problem with crossing the large field, Point 2 can be reached by continuing along the B5009 to the next junction. Turn off to the right, then proceed along the narrow lane to the next junction and fork left; this is Point 2. For the adventurous, cross the stile to the first field, proceed to the far left corner and cross a stile into the large field (careful, shallow ditch beyond). Now go part right and aim for an electricity pole visually located between two pylons, (compass bearing 27°, magnetic). On reaching this continue in the same direction now aiming for a stile in the hedge, about 100 yards left of the farm buildings. Cross this stile to a lane and turn left. At a road junction turn right.

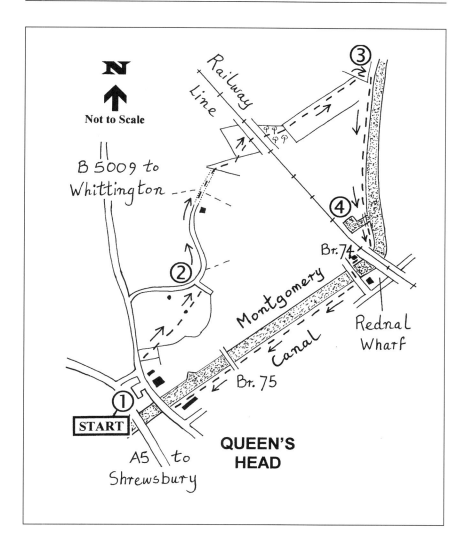

2. Continue along the narrow lane which, after several hundred yards, becomes a wide grassy track. At the end of the track cross a stile by a gate (careful, deep ditch to the left), then follow the left fence/hedge and a water filled ditch, to the next stile, about 150 yards. Care again needed in crossing two stiles either side of the ditch. Then, having negotiated a nettle patch, turn part right and cross the field to a stile in the tree/hedge line ahead, about one third in from the right edge of the field. Now cross the main railway line between Shrewsbury and Wrexham, observing the signs (trains now go somewhat faster than 150 years ago). Once over the track go down and through a wood to a ditch crossing, which might be hidden by undergrowth, and cross a stile to a field. Follow the left field edge to a stile at the far end, cross this and turn right to another stile and then to the towpath of the Montgomery Canal.

3. Turn right at the towpath and follow this tranquil section of canal (on the left) to reach a small canal arm that leads to a larger canal basin. This was a railway and canal interchange point which had its own railway sidings. Here goods could be transferred between narrow boat and goods wagons for distribution as required. Subsequently there was a fertiliser factory here, demolished in the 1960s, where animal bones were crushed to make fertiliser for the farms. It was known locally as the 'bone factory' and locals remember it, with affection, as a great source of maggots for fishing.

4. Having explored the canal arm, continue over the swing bridge (after about 100 yards note the canal 'mile post' on the towpath) and then under the railway bridge (the same line as crossed earlier). Immediately under the bridge the restored, part timber-framed, building on the opposite canal bank is the Rednal Wharf and Warehouse. Apart from being a place to store goods for loading/unloading for canal transportation, it is also believed to be the local 'station' of a short-lived passenger service. Immediately beyond Rednal Wharf is Bridge 74, a classic example of a roving bridge. The sweep in this bridge shows how the horse could change from one side of the canal to the other without the tow-rope being unhitched. Having crossed the bridge continue along the towpath (canal now on the right), going under bridge 75 to reach the site of the old Queen's Head Wharf. Then cross Bridge 76 back to the car park.

Those who wish to add Walk 8 to this walk, without visiting the pub, just continue on the canal towpath.

PLACES OF INTEREST NEARBY
Nesscliffe Hill Country Park is situated near the A5 at Nesscliffe village, about midway between Oswestry and Shrewsbury. Nesscliffe Hill is a sandstone escarpment covered by mixed woodlands. Phone the Tourist Information Centre on 01743 350761 for further details.

MAESBURY WHARF AND THE MONTGOMERY CANAL

This interesting and varied walk combines something of a medieval pilgrimage, passing the site of a Norman castle and visiting a Holy Well, with a look at a late 18th century canal and wharf.

Maesbury Wharf

It is the older part of West Felton that is included in this walk, a picturesque area of old cottages, a church dating back to the 12th century, and the remains of a Norman fortification. Further west is the hamlet of Woolston which is the site of St Winifred's Well, a spring that in medieval times was reputed to have healing powers, particularly for the eyes. The well at Woolston still flows out from beneath a half timbered building, administered by The Landmark Trust, that was built much later, possibly on the orders of Lady Margaret Beaufort, mother of Henry VII, who arranged the building of the Beaufort Chapel at Holywell. From the Well, the walk returns to Queen's Head along the Montgomery Canal from Maesbury Marsh, a section which includes the three Aston Locks (restored 1996/7). Maesbury Wharf was the main wharf for the transit of goods to, and from, Oswestry.

On the canal at Maesbury Marsh is the Navigation Inn, a restored 17th century coaching inn with low beams in the dining area. In the bar a drink can be enjoyed sitting in some French 18th century choir stalls from Dromfor, Normandy. When the canal is not fully operational lunchtime opening (food from 12 noon to 2 pm) is on Friday to Sunday only. However, it is open all week in the evening (food from 7 pm to 9.30 pm). A range of 'Good Pub Fare' is offered, including filled baguettes, jacket potatoes, lasagne, grills and fish dishes such as smoked haddock. Being a free house there is always a range of beers, lagers, ciders and wine available, to quench the thirst, or stimulate the palate, of the weary traveller. Telephone: 01691 672958. Also, at the start point, there is The Queen's Head (see the notes in Walk 7).

- **HOW TO GET THERE:** Queen's Head is located just off the A5 (junction with the B5009), some 4 miles south-east of Oswestry.
- **PARKING:** Car park (and picnic tables) by the canal opposite The Queen's Head.
- **LENGTH OF THE WALK:** 6 miles. It can be linked with Walk 7 to make a 9 mile walk. Map: OS Explorer 240 Oswestry (GR 339268).

THE WALK

1. From the car park turn right, along the road and over the bridge, then right again to join the canal towpath. The road was once the old A5, The Queen's Head inn being a welcome refreshment stop for both road and canal travellers. Continue along the towpath passing Aston Top Lock the first of three in the Aston Flight, and proceed to just past the second lock. Here turn left to cross two stiles with a ditch crossing between. (This path is the second one going left by the lock, the first is about the centre point of the lock but was not used as there is a steep descent to the stile and it can be very muddy.)

2. Now follow the left edge of the field, cross a stile in the hedge ahead and proceed directly over the next field, (timber-framed house ahead/left). Cross a stile in the left hedge, just prior to

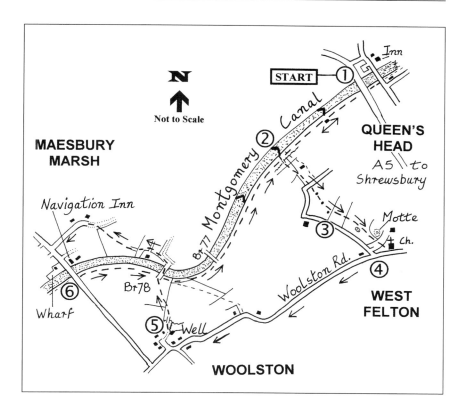

reaching a fence. Note the interesting dog-gate in the stile. Once over continue in the same direction, hedge to the right, to reach a stile to a lane. The area just crossed is named Cupid's Ramble on OS maps! Cross the lane to the stile opposite and prepare to walk across an arable field. (If there are problems at this point with crops turn right at the lane and follow it to West Felton, Point 4, please see map.) Once in the field go part right and aim for the first electricity pole, proceed directly to the second pole, then aim to the left of the third. Soon a stile should be visible in the hedge ahead, aim for this and cross (or go around) it.

3. Now go directly across the next field, cross a loose barbed wire fence at an old hedge line (there could be a stile by the time you walk this way) and continue over the next field passing to the left of a group of trees around a pond. At the far end of the field go

The pub at Maesbury Marsh

through a metal gate. The tree-covered mound to the left is the site
of a Norman motte. Go across the wide farm track and over a stile
to the churchyard. Proceed through the churchyard to the road (St
Michael's church is usually locked). Turn right and reach the road
junction with the lane crossed earlier in the walk.

4. The route is now along the road towards Woolston and Maesbury
Marsh (Woolston Road), and allows some brisk road walking for
about 1½ miles. From the road there are good open views. Enter
the village of Woolston, follow the road as it sweeps right and at the
next bend (road sweeping left), keep straight ahead on a gravel
lane. The sign 'Private Drive — Residents Only' refers to cars, the
lane is an access, on foot, to St Winifred's Well. At the lane end turn
right, go through a gate, and follow the path down to a building on
the right. This is St Winifred's Well. Whilst access has been allowed
to view the well, the building and grounds are private, so please
respect this. The route for the walk continues past the well and
through the trees at the bottom right of the small lawn, partly
hidden until you find it. Follow the path to a footbridge over the
stream.

5. Once over the footbridge cross a stile and then a boggy area with an assortment of stepping bricks and logs. Follow the left hedge, cross a stile by a gate, then go across the corner of the field to reach a bridge over the canal. Continue over the bridge, now on a bridlepath, following the path into a field and turn left. Now follow the left fence (ignoring the track as it sweeps right), cross a stile by a gate and continue following the left fence. Use a bridlegate, or stile, to a drive, cross the stile opposite, then go part left over the field corner to stiles with a footbridge between. In the next field go part right, up a bank, then head towards the buildings visible beyond the far left corner of the field. Join a track via a gate, turn left, and follow the lane to the road junction. Here turn left and follow the road to the canal bridge, the Navigation Inn, left, and the old Maesbury Wharf, right.

6. Having satisfied both the thirsts of body and for knowledge, join the canal towpath and go east, canal on the left, passing The Navigation Inn on the opposite bank. This currently little used section of canal is still a haven for wild life and wild flowers. Also, because the canal is not in constant use, reeds can quickly take over the waterway and need clearing regularly. The journey back to Queen's Head is a pleasant and relaxing walk, first under Bridge 78 (the bridge crossed earlier in the walk), passing a winding hole (a narrow boat turning point) on the opposite bank, then under Bridge 77 to reach Aston Bottom Lock. At the lock notice the new mile post, even if directionally it would be more appropriate on the opposite bank. Continue on the canal towpath to the middle lock, the point this walk left the canal, and on past the top lock back to the start.

PLACES OF INTEREST NEARBY

As this walk starts from the same point as Walk 7 please see the relevant section in that Walk.

RIVER AND CANAL AT LLANYMYNECH

❦

A varied walk with constantly changing views that includes a meandering river, field paths, quiet country roads, the Montgomery Canal, disused railway lines and old lime kilns. Something for everyone!

The River Vyrnwy

Llanymynech (the local shop will advise you how to pronounce it!) is a place of considerable antiquity and significant industrial past. The village is dominated by Llanymynech Hill, with its vast deposits of limestone. The disused quarries are now a nature reserve and within the village is a Heritage Area where the industrial past can be explored.

The River Vyrnwy (or Afon Efyrnwy, its Welsh name) nearby is really a tributary of the River Severn, and from Llanymynech to Melverley it is, more or less, the Welsh/English border. However, its meandering course and water flow did not lend itself to navigation. The Montgomery Canal has been partially restored (but is not yet fully navigable) from Llanymynech westwards into Wales, a major feat seeing that the canal was abandoned in 1944.

In Llanymynech itself there are four hostelries, one in Wales, two in England, and one 'half and half'. My choice for a meal was The Bradford Arms and Restaurant (mainly because I love food and this is a restaurant with a bar rather than an inn with a restaurant). The range of food and wine available is very extensive with dishes from around the world, there is also a well stocked bar. After a hard day of walking the goat's cheese, followed by guinea fowl, and digested with some good claret, went down very well. It is open from Tuesday to Sunday, lunch is 12 noon to 2 pm and evening from 7 pm to 10 pm (9 pm on Sunday). Telephone: 01691 830582.

- **HOW TO GET THERE:** Llanymynech is situated on the A483 about 6 miles south of Oswestry.
- **PARKING:** Public car park (in Wales) accessed off the B4398 via an entrance between the post office and The Dolphin.
- **LENGTH OF THE WALK:** 2$\frac{1}{2}$ miles or 7 miles. Maps: OS Explorer 240 Oswestry (GR 266209).

THE WALK

1. From the car park entrance turn left to reach the A483, there turn right, cross the road when convenient, and pass the Bradford Arms and the Lion Hotel. Turn left into Rectory Lane, passing the parish church of St Agatha. Continue along Rectory Lane and, when it sweeps left, go right, on an enclosed tarmac drive, then down a gravel slope to a stile. In the field first go slightly right and then sweep left to cross another stile. Go over an abandoned Cambrian Railways line, through a gap in the hedge, then go part left and reach the bank of the River Vyrnwy. At this point the pillars in the river are the remains of a railway bridge. Continue past the bridge buttress, go through a gate, then cross the end of the field to a gap in the fence. Now go part right to another gap in the hedge, turn left and, after about 50 yards, go through a gate on the left. Cross the field walking parallel to the hedge over on the left, with a wonderful view, left, of the Llanymynech Cliffs. At the far side of the field enter, via a gate, an old green lane and follow this to reach, via another gate, the B4398. Here turn right.

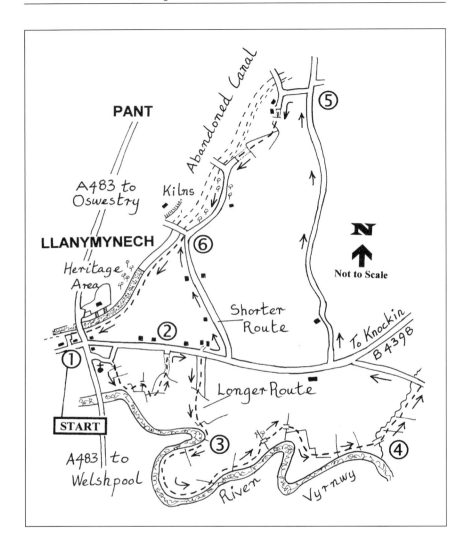

2. SHORTER WALK: Continue along the B4398 to reach the next road on the left, signposted Pant. Follow this road to the canal bridge at Point 6 and then continue with the route notes from there.

LONGER WALK: Proceed along the B4398 for some 300 yards, passing a house on the left and reaching, also on the left, a number of large barns. At a point opposite the drive to the barns go through a gate on the right. Now go across the long field to a gate at the far

St Agatha's church, Llanymynech

right corner and, once through, turn part left to cross this field to another gate. On reaching the next gate go through and join a wide track which sweeps right to another gate, the path now following the course of the River Vyrnwy.

3. The route now keeps to the right of the field following the course of the river, passing through more gateways and then over some horse jumps with stiles (or use the bridlegate). The route here is also used for point to point meetings. After passing the horse jumps with the stiles the route goes between two large trees, and then crosses a bridge over a wide ditch. Just beyond the bridge pass under some electricity cables and then continue straight ahead, moving away from the river bank. Soon cross another bridge then, after some 40 yards, go through a gate on the right. Now go part left towards the tree line ahead, to a point between the hedge corner (left) and a dyke (right). Follow the dyke to a stile in a hedge then continue ahead to rejoin the river bank. Now follow the river bank, crossing two more stiles, before following the line of a dyke to reach a footbridge over a stream.

4. Cross the footbridge and immediately turn left over a stile, then follow the top of another dyke as it sweeps left and right, stream to the left, to cross three more stiles to reach a lane. Here turn left. The route is now along the lane to the B4398, then turn left and, after 100 yards, take the next road right, signposted Chickheath and Morton. The route is now a pleasant, easy walk along a country lane for just over 1 mile to the next road junction, then turn left.

5. Having turned left follow the road for some 300 yards to where it sweeps right. Now continue ahead on a narrower lane, signposted as a bridlepath. On reaching a farm sweep left to go through a gate, keeping all farm buildings on the right. Go across a short open space to join a hedge on the right, go through a gate, over a field, then through another gate and turn right. Follow the right edge of this large field to a gate at the far right corner. Go through onto a track and eventually reach a road junction. Here keep left (the right turn is to a canal bridge) and follow the road, passing the buttresses of a demolished railway bridge, to reach a bridge over the canal.

6. Now join the canal towpath (either side of the bridge), and turn left to follow the line of the canal. Pass the buttress of a dismantled railway bridge and then reach a part of the canal now filled with water. From here the tall chimney visible across the canal was for the Hoffman Ring Kiln for producing quicklime; it is situated at the Heritage Area. Continue along the towpath, passing the Heritage Area on the opposite bank (notice the small canal arms for loading the narrowboats). Pass under the A483 and then cross a stile back to the car park.

PLACES OF INTEREST NEARBY
In Llanymynech itself, at the junction of the A483 and the canal, is the *Heritage Area* which is on the site of the old lime processing works, a great place to explore for anyone interested in industrial archaeology. At the top of Llanymynech Hill is the *Llanymynech Rocks Nature Reserve*, consisting of the old quarry area, Roman mine workings and Offa's Dyke. Then, a little further north, just beyond Pant, is the *Llynclys Common Nature Reserve*, another hill top area with limestone grasslands and established woodland.

WALK 10

THE RIVER VYRNWY AND
THE RIVER SEVERN

*Two short walks for the price of one, linking the Vyrnwy and Severn
rivers. With a 600 year old wooden church and an inn, both walks
give sweeping views over north Shropshire.*

The River Severn at Melverley

The hamlet of Melverley is almost enfolded by two rivers, the
Vyrnwy and the Severn. At its centre is an architectural gem, the
15th century church of St Peter. Dominating the hamlet are the hills
collectively known as 'The Breiddens', Breidden Hill itself being
crowned by Rodney's Pillar, a monument erected in 1781 to Admiral
Rodney. At Melverley the Severn, the longest river in Britain, is
joined by the Vyrnwy, and dykes (called Argaes by the locals) have
been constructed over the years to minimise the risk of flooding,
these now providing the basis for many footpaths in the area. Also
encountered is the Severn Way, a new 210 mile long distance path.

Situated within sight of the church is the Tontine Inn. The term 'Tontine' apparently originates from one Lorenzo Tonti, a Neapolitan banker, and is a scheme whereby several participants pay towards a lump sum, which provides annual interest to those still alive and then the last one takes what is left. (This sort of scheme should have carried a health warning!) However, the visitor to the Tontine Inn today will be rewarded with good healthy food which can be washed down with Bass, Worthington or the current 'guest' beer. The food range includes meat grills, various chicken dishes (garlic and Cajun), and also 'home made' specialities (the steak and kidney pie was the old style, made in a large dish and cut into slices). Food is served every day, lunch is 12.30 pm to 2 pm, and evening meals from 6.30 pm to 9 pm. Telephone: 01691 682258.

- **HOW TO GET THERE:** Melverley is situated 1 mile north of Crew Green, which is on the B4393 to the west of Shrewsbury.
- **PARKING:** There is a limited amount of verge parking on the left of the lane between the Tontine Inn and the church; this could be busy on Sundays. There is alternative parking at a large lay-by just north of the bridge over the Severn from Crew Green, and if this is used the walk can be started from Point 6.
- **LENGTH OF THE WALK:** $2^1/_2$ or 5 miles. Map: OS Explorer 240 Oswestry (GR 333166).

THE WALK

1. Enter the churchyard from the lane, turn right, leave the churchyard via a gate, and follow the top of a small dyke, the River Vyrnwy on the left. Shortly after crossing the third stile (ignore the footpath going right, this is for the return journey) look for a group of buildings on the opposite bank (Haim). At this point the river has been realigned to try and reduce the flooding problems. After passing Haim follow the dyke over three more stiles (ignore another footpath going right) and reach a farm track.

2. Cross the farm track then, immediately after crossing the stile opposite, turn right and down the bank to cross a stile to an arable field. Cross the field to a stile in the opposite hedge, about the mid point of the largest gap between the trees. Continue over the next field to a ditch crossing with stiles, then cross two more fields to enter a lane and turn right. Follow the lane passing a farm on the

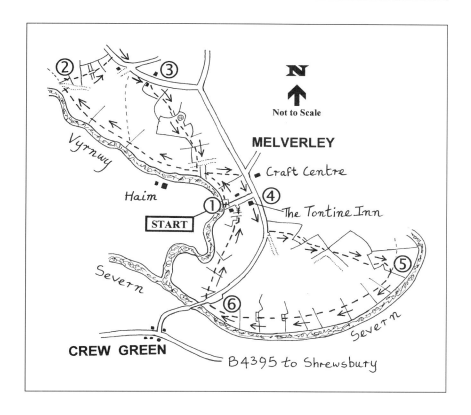

right. Pass a dirt track (right) and then take the tarmac lane going right, ignoring the footpath to the right. Continue along the lane for some 200 yards to reach a stile on the right, opposite a house.

3. Having crossed the stile go part left, cross a stile by the field corner and proceed to a ditch crossing and stile in the opposite hedge. Now pass a pond, and then a hedge corner on the left. Continue through a gap in a hedge (a culvert bridge over a ditch), then follow the right hedge to a stile in the field corner. Cross the next field to reach a dirt track, crossing this to rejoin the dyke. There turn left, cross the two stiles about 50 yards apart, and then go part left, leaving the dyke, to a stile in the far corner of the field. Having crossed turn right and follow the lane, passing the Craft Centre on the left to reach the Tontine Inn. Time for a break?

4. If you are carrying on for the full walk, from the inn take the road going towards Crew Green (see map), following it to the point where it sweeps right, a narrow lane going ahead. Here cross a stile on the left, hidden behind a roadside 'Sharp Deviation' sign. Cross the field, keeping mid way between the electricity poles, to a stile in the opposite fence. Continue over the next field and cross a ditch crossing, fence and a stile, then go part left and exit the field by a gate in the far corner. Go over the junction of two farm tracks to a stile by a metal gate. The path over this next field is part right to a stile in the far hedge. However, the farmer sometimes cuts a path through any crops around the outside of the field, so you may have a choice. Once over the field cross another ditch crossing and stile, then go part left to reach the corner of a hedge. Here go part right to reach a dyke and turn right to follow it.

5. The route for the walk is now along the dyke, built to try and contain the River Severn in times of flood, the river being over to the left. Continue along the dyke, going over twelve stiles to reach the bridge over the Severn. Cross the stile to its right and join the road at a large lay-by.

6. Before continuing the walk take a little time to notice the bridge, from which the confluence of the rivers Vyrnwy and Severn is clearly visible. This was once a railway bridge on the line of the Breidden Branch of the Shrewsbury and North Wales Railway. To continue the walk pass through the tree line (by the end of the bridge opposite the lay-by) and cross a stile. The route from here to Melverley is part of the Severn Way and follows yet another dyke. Follow the dyke crossing three more stiles and coming close to the Vyrnwy. On approaching farm buildings keep to the right of the hedge and follow it around to a stile. Cross into the farm area and proceed, towards the right, to a stile by a gate. From here continue to the lane which is the start point of the walk.

PLACES OF INTEREST NEARBY
Near the Tontine Inn is the *Melverley Craft Centre*, open on Fridays, Saturdays and Sundays. Only 10 miles away is *Shrewsbury*, with its museums, gardens, churches and abbey. Further details available from the Tourist Information Centre on 01743 350761.

PONTESBURY AND TWO BROOKS

This walk along the Kingfisher Way visits two smaller brooks located in the Rea Valley, a pastoral location situated between two hill ranges, the Breiddens and Long Mountain to the north-west, and the Long Mynd and Stiperstones to the south.

Pontesford Brook

Pontesbury lies in an area that has been occupied since ancient times, evidenced by the earthworks on the adjacent hills. Connections with the Norman occupation now rely on records of a castle that occupied land to the west of the church, since no physical trace now remains. This short walk leaves Pontesbury to follow some very small brooks, some paths being on the Kingfisher Way, a waymarked route between Shrewsbury and Pontesbury along the Rea Valley. The Pontesford Brook flows northward from near Earl's Hill to join the Rea Brook which, in turn, flows north-eastward along the Rea Valley to join the River Severn at Shrewsbury. This Rea Brook is different to the one mentioned in Walk 18.

One of the most noticeable buildings when entering Pontesbury on the A488 from the east, right at the start of the one-way system, is the Red Lion with its colourful array of hanging baskets. It is well used by the local people and that is always a good sign. The house speciality is grilled steaks and their mixed grill, and there are also the usual range of bar snacks (lasagne, fish, etc), as well as vegetarian choices. The main beer range is Tetley and Worthington and there is always a 'guest beer' as well as lager and cider. Food hours are 12 noon to 2 pm and 7 pm to 9 pm, all week. With a choice of two bars and a dining area this is a good place to start (or finish) the walk. Telephone: 01743 790321.

- **HOW TO GET THERE:** Pontesbury is situated on the A488 Shrewsbury to Bishops Castle road, some 8 miles south west of Shrewsbury.
- **PARKING:** On road parking is available on the one-way system by the shops near the church (School Bank and Main Street). This is also the parking area used by local people for shopping.
- **LENGTH OF THE WALK:** 3 or 4 miles. Map: OS Explorer 216 Welshpool & Montgomery, also 241 Shrewsbury (GR 399061).

THE WALK

1. From the start point in School Bank (by the newsagent's and the church) follow the traffic flow into Main Street and at the junction turn right into Hall Bank. After 50 yards turn left over a stile, joining part of the Kingfisher Way. Cross the field, digressing slightly away from the left fence, to cross another stile in the tree-line opposite. Cross over a path to a children's play area to cross a stile and footbridge over a brook. The track just crossed is on the line of a now dismantled railway, the Minsterley Branch of the Shrewsbury and Welshpool Branch Railway. Once over the brook turn part right and head towards metal gates in the far corner of the field. Take the path to the left of the fence, around the perimeter of the sewage works, with a small brook on the left. On the other side cross a footbridge and follow the left hedge, and the brook, passing through the line of an old hedge. Here the prominent high ground to the right/rear is the tree-covered Pontesford Hill with Earl's Hill immediately behind. Cross a culvert bridge over a brook and turn part right to follow the brook to a footbridge (a choice of two in fact, a safe one or a more adventurous one). Proceed to a stile to a

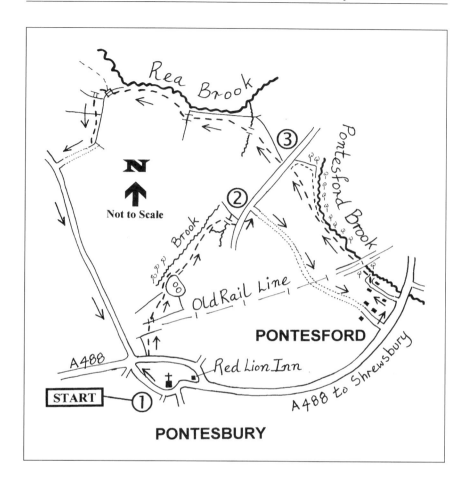

lane, then go left, along the lane, for some 75 yards to a bridlepath going right. Now for the choice of walk length. For the longer walk see Point 2 below, for the shorter walk follow the road for a further 300 yards to a stile by a gate on the left, then continue the walk from Point 3.

2. For the longer walk turn right along the unmade bridlepath (an old green lane), with a good view ahead of wooded Pontesford Hill. Continue across the old railway route crossed earlier and on reaching the A488 turn left, following the road for some 200 yards to the bridge over the Pontesford Brook. Do not cross the bridge but

55

turn left, up a tarmac drive, with the Pontesford Brook (and footbridges) on the right. The drive is a public footpath and continues through the courtyard of a house and into the garden. (Whilst it is a right of way please respect the privacy of the owners.) Once in the garden keep right to rejoin the brook and follow it to the end of the garden and through a gap in the conifer trees. Follow the path, crossing two stiles and then go through a pedestrian tunnel under the old railway line. Keep the brook close on the right and enter a large arable field. It is now a case of following the brook by keeping to the right edge of the field. About 200 yards into the field the map shows the right of way going across the field to the road. However, unless the path is marked out (most unlikely) or you are an expert with map and compass, the best solution is to keep to the right edge of the field. From here the view ahead is of the Breidden Hills, Rodney's Pillar to the right. The exit point, a gap to the road in the far hedge, is only about 100 yards from the very far end of the field. Having reached the road, turn left and almost immediately cross a stile on the right, by a gate.

3. Once in the field go directly across it to a footbridge and in the next field take a line that converges with the fence on the right, to join the Rea Brook. Proceed to the corner of the field, following the brook, and cross yet another stile and footbridge, then repeat the exercise in the next field, this time with two stiles and a footbridge between. Now turn left and soon cross yet more stiles with a footbridge between. This section was well waymarked but a little overgrown through lack of use. Cross a narrow field to a stile in the opposite left corner, partly hidden by a tree, then follow the left side of the field for about 250 yards to a stile on the left. Now join a farm track, turn right and follow the track to a lane. Here turn left and follow the lane back into Pontesbury.

PLACES OF INTEREST NEARBY

Immediately south of Pontesbury is *Poles Coppice*, a reserve of mixed woodland and old quarries, now administered by Shropshire County Council. Due east of Poles Coppice is the *Earl's Hill Nature Reserve*, administered by the Shropshire Wildlife Trust, with its Iron Age hill fort, mixed woodland and acid grassland.

THE RIVER SEVERN AT IRONBRIDGE

Truly a walk of variety, starting from the cradle of the Industrial Revolution, Ironbridge, that includes the Iron Bridge itself, Benthall Edge Wood with its heavily coppiced trees, the River Severn and a visit (optional) to the medieval ruins of Buildwas Abbey.

The famous Iron Bridge

The area covered by this walk is steeped in history, both natural and man made. It was in this location, over 10,000 years ago that the great lake north of Wenlock Edge burst through between the Edge and the Wrekin, forming what is now the Ironbridge Gorge. The woodland and mineral deposits, particularly coal and limestone, attracted people to the gorge, resulting in a flourishing iron, pottery and tile industry developing. It was here, in 1709, that Abraham Derby I finally succeeded in effectively producing iron using coke instead of charcoal, thereby increasing the rate at which iron could be produced. Ironbridge now takes its name from the construction, in 1777/78, of the world's first major iron bridge.

Near the start of the walk, just past the Museum of the Gorge, is The Malthouse, which promotes itself as a 'restaurant with rooms' and a pub. The restaurant offers a wide range of meals such as steaks, fowl (duck) and fish (red mullet), and the 'pub' area has substantial bar meals, such as grilled salmon, liver and onions, tagliatelle carbonara, etc. The coffee in the 'pub' section comes in French 'breakfast sized' cups. The beers on offer include Bass, Flowers and Tetley, there are also lagers and cider and a good wine list. All in all, a good place for a meal either before, or after, the walk. Food is available from 12 noon to 2 pm and 7 pm to 9.30 pm, all week. Telephone: 01952 433712.

- **HOW TO GET THERE:** Ironbridge is situated to the south of Telford and can be approached from all points of the compass. As it is now a major tourist attraction it is well signposted, just follow the signs to the 'Ironbridge Gorge and Museums'.
- **PARKING:** Most car parks in Ironbridge are short stay so the one chosen here is the long stay car park by the Dale End Park, on the Buildwas Road to the west of the Town Centre.
- **LENGTH OF THE WALK:** 5 miles. Map: OS Explorer 242 Telford, Ironbridge & The Wrekin (GR 664037).

THE WALK

1. Leave the car park by walking towards the river, then turn left and follow the riverside path, passing the Antiques Centre. Reach the road by the Museum of the Gorge, the area here being the site of an old wharf. Turn right along the road, part of the Severn Way, and follow it to reach the Iron Bridge. The main centre is by the bridge itself and that is worth closer inspection. When ready, cross the bridge and take time to visit the Toll House (free entry) before continuing with the walk, if you still have enough time left!

2. From the Toll House go to the end of the bridge, turn right onto an unmade track (note the old Severn Valley Railway lines still in position in the road) and follow it, the river to the right. (The 'No Public Right of Way' sign refers to the path going under the bridge.) Proceed along the track passing a number of renovated cottages as it rises gently to reach an underpass under a bridge, the old SVR line.

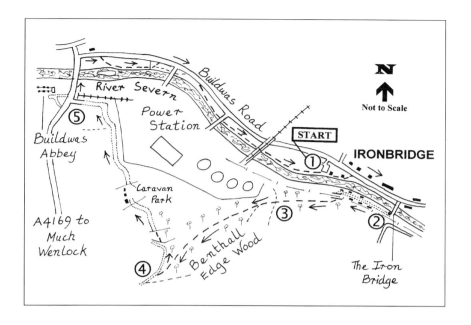

Go under the bridge and immediately turn right, then follow the path with the steps going uphill into Benthall Edge Wood. These woods show extensive signs of coppicing, the resulting smaller stems from the base root being used for charcoal making, pit props, etc. The whole area here was mined for coal and quarried for stone, as well as providing wood, so leave the marked path at your peril. As the path gently rises, with several level portions, there are good views, right, of the Severn Gorge with the River Severn down below, the extent of the view depending on the time of year and the foliage. At a point where the path dips the apparent sound of a waterfall may be audible, but this is from the cooling towers of Ironbridge Power Station. At this point a junction of paths is reached. From the Iron Bridge to here is part of the Shropshire Way.

3. At the path junction take the wide path going part left and sloping gently uphill (not the path with the steps), signposted Benthall. Follow the path, cooling towers now on the right, and when the path forks keep right. As the path goes uphill it becomes, in parts, narrower. At a point where there is a clearing on the right the view is across the Severn Valley. Proceed on the path and soon a wide track appears down to the right. Continue until the two paths meet, then turn sharp right and onto the wide, downhill track.

4. Proceed downhill, viewing the full glory of the cooling towers, as the path sweeps gently left. Where the wide track goes sharp left go straight ahead, first on a narrow path and then joining a wide track through a young tree plantation. Continue under the electric cables and pass a bungalow on the left to enter the Pool View Caravan Park. Follow the rough track through the caravan park to reach railway lines ahead. Here turn left and follow it to the A4169.

5. On reaching the A4169, a visit to Buildwas Abbey, a Cistercian abbey founded in 1135, on the opposite side of the road is possible. The ruins are administered by English Heritage and are open from 10 am to 6 pm, April to October. The route of the walk, however, is right and over the River Severn. Turn right, towards Ironbridge, immediately after crossing the bridge. Follow the road for about 200 yards then cross a stile on the right to follow the riverside path. But, before continuing, go across to the river bank opposite the gate and stile. The channel here, between the bank and the island, is probably a 'barge gutter', allowing craft to pass easily through. Now it is a case of following the Severn Way back to the starting point. However, a word of caution. At the time of writing, in the summer of 1999, there had been a land slip beneath the first bridge of the three between here and Ironbridge. It is therefore suggested that after the next stile (about 150 yards from the first bridge) the left fork in the path, to the road, is taken. Follow the road for some 450 yards, then rejoin the Severn Way and riverside path at a gap in the hedge (not at the stile passed on the way). The route then goes under the road bridge to the Power Station, then under the Albert Edward Bridge, past the Ironbridge Rowing Club and through the Dale End Park back to the car park.

PLACES OF INTEREST NEARBY
Ironbridge is an outstanding area of industrial heritage with eight museums, covering the gorge, iron making, tile manufacture, china and a recreated Victorian town, as well as a Visitor and Tourist Information Centre. Telephone: 01952 432166.

FROM BRIDGNORTH BY RIVER AND BROOK

❧❧

The walk starts at the historic town of Bridgnorth and follows the Severn Way with dramatic views across the Severn, then sweeps away from the river, through woods and the picturesque village of Astley Abbotts, and back along the wooded Cantern Brook.

Boldings Fishing Pools near Astley Abbotts

Bridgnorth is one of those places that it is always a joy to visit – a bustling market town with fascinating old buildings, a ruined castle, the Severn Valley Railway, and so much more. All in all an ideal place for a riverside walk. Bridgnorth was once a bustling inland port, records showing that it was a major loading point for pottery brought down from the Stoke on Trent area. In direct contrast to the River Severn is the Cantern Brook, a small brook that rises to the west of Astley Abbotts and offers a peaceful waterside walk, through woods, before rejoining the hustle and bustle of Bridgnorth.

Although this is an excellent riverside walk, there are no hostelries on the route, so flexible food times at Bridgnorth are important. In the High Street is The Crown, a deceptively spacious building, much larger and older than the High Street entrance indicates (Dr Who would like this place). Good food, and a good range of beers and wines, is available all day from 10 am up to 9.30 pm, this from a menu that ranges from sandwiches and baguettes to salads and meals from around the world. Telephone: 01746 763229.

- **HOW TO GET THERE:** Bridgnorth is located at the junction of the A442 and the A458.
- **PARKING:** For this walk it is advisable to use one of the long stay car parks. These are in Old Smithfield, at the rear of the Somerfield Supermarket, and at Innage Lane (the cheaper one on a Saturday) by the Fire Station, both are signposted.
- **LENGTH OF THE WALK:** 7 miles. Map: OS Explorer 218 Wyre Forest & Kidderminster (GR 716932).

THE WALK

1. From the Town Hall, built in 1652 after the Civil War, walk down the High Street passing The Swan, a 17th-century coaching inn, on the left. On reaching Waterloo Terrace turn left into Cartway, so called as it was the route for carts and packhorses conveying goods between the river and High Town. Proceed down Cartway and, where it goes right, go directly ahead into Friar's Street. Before continuing along Friar's Street take a walk across the grassed area on the right for a superb view of the River Severn and High Rock. After about 100 yards along the street, take the steps going down to the right, Friar's Loade. At the bottom of the steps turn left and soon reach the remains of a medieval Franciscan friary. Continue along the road to go through a kissing gate into a playing field.

2. The walk now follows the Severn Way (look for the Severn Trow symbol) for almost 3 miles along the Severn, crossing two footbridges and eight stiles, including the footbridge ones. At the first footbridge, over the Cantern Brook, the sandstone outcrop on the opposite bank is High Rock, a wonderful vantage point for viewing Bridgnorth and the river (but not for the nervous!). The route continues to follow the river through a golf course (watch out for wayward balls!), and then into fields. In time higher ground

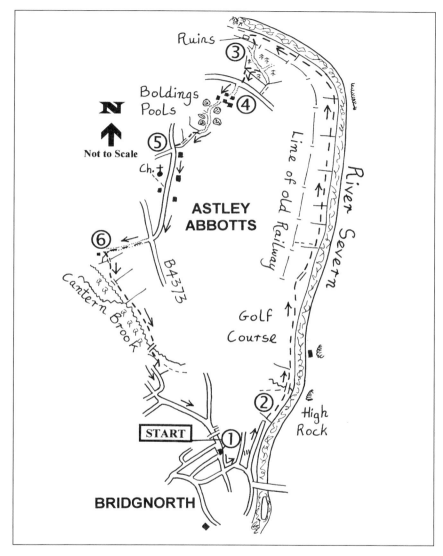

appears over to the right, with glimpses of more sandstone cliffs and a cave. After the river sweeps left leave a field to walk between the old SVR track and the river, then, as the distance between them widens, go some 50 yards past a stile and gate on the left.

3. At this point, on the left, are the remains of an old dwelling,

Bridgnorth on market day

partly built into the sandstone cliff and almost certainly associated with the river. One old 19th-century map indicates that there was a ferry near this point and a track on the opposite bank going to Apley Park. Now retrace your steps back to the gate and stile (now on the right), cross the stile, cross the line of the old SVR, and take the wide path opposite. Follow this, first uphill and then on a more level section. Just prior to a slight uphill section, at a path junction with wide paths going ahead and left, take a narrow path going up into the trees on the right. (If you miss this turn off just follow the wider path, through a field, to reach the road and then turn right, please see the map.) The narrow track meanders upwards through the trees to a stile. Once over go across the field, the path should be marked but, if not, just aim well to the left of the buildings ahead. On reaching a road turn right then, after only 40 yards, turn left down a drive marked Boldings Pools.

4. Proceed down the drive (it is a right of way but, at the time of writing, no finger post or waymark signs were visible), and pass between the first two large sheds. Now turn right, again between sheds, and immediately past the one on the left, turn left. Now go ahead to join a wide track and follow it, between fishing pools, as it first goes ahead then turns left, and eventually leaves the pools to cross a field. Follow this grassy track as it meanders through conifers to a stile and, once over, turn left and follow the left fence. Cross a narrow footbridge, with stiles, and continue along the left fence to a lane and turn left.

5. The route is now through the quiet and scattered village of Astley Abbotts passing the small church of St Calixtus. Continue along the lane, now with a panoramic view, left, towards Staffordshire. On reaching the B4373 cross it and take the concrete track opposite that passes the village hall. This eventually becomes a stony track with the good view, ahead/left, of Brown Clee Hill with its radio masts. Continue along the path to reach some iron gates supported by two large sandstone gateposts.

6. Continue past the gateposts, immediately turn left and through a gate, then cross the end of a lawn to reach a field via a stile (this is the official right of way). Now cross the field to the opposite hedge and cross a footbridge with stiles. The route here is now part right and across the field to the far right corner but, as there is no obvious aiming point, most people just turn right and follow the right side of the field to eventually reach a stile. Here cross another footbridge with stiles and again follow the right edge of the field, a small brook to the right. This path is not as shown on the OS map but is the route as marked by the County Council. Cross another stile into woodland, the Cantern Brook now down to the right, and follow the meandering, undulating and often muddy path to reach a concrete footbridge over the brook. Having crossed over turn left and after about 25 yards take the right fork that goes uphill to meet a wooden fence. Follow the fence to a grassed area, go up to the estate road, and turn left. Follow the road as it sweeps right to a road junction by shops. Here turn left, soon join another road, then keep ahead to return to Bridgnorth Town Centre.

PLACES OF INTEREST NEARBY
Bridgnorth itself is a place that justifies more than one visit, having a wealth of old buildings and walkways to see and explore. Full details are available from the Tourist Information Centre in Listley Street. Telephone: 01746 763257.

WALK 14
THE SEVERN VALLEY: RIVER AND RAILWAY

Another walk from the historic town of Bridgnorth, with panoramic views along the Severn Valley, but this time one that should please steam train enthusiasts as well as riverside ramblers.

The sandstone cliff at Quatford

Oldbury is now part of Bridgnorth and it is an attractive village with most of the houses hidden away behind the main road. South-east of Oldbury lies Eardington, which was recorded as having a mill in Saxon times.

At one time the Severn played a significant part in the life of the area, but eventually replacing the river as the main form of transport was the Severn Valley Railway, which operated from 1862 until its closure (progressively) between 1963 and 1969. However, by 1966 the new Severn Valley Railway had come into being and now operates between Kidderminster and Bridgnorth.

The Halfway House Inn specialises in good food, real ales and boasts that it has at least 40 malt whiskies and over 100 wines. It also specialises in 'stag' and 'hen' weekends, so can be quite busy then. The sign outside says it is a 'Ham and Eggery' so what else could I have – superb thick ham and fresh, lightly fried, eggs. As the inn also has accommodation the owner requests that muddy boots are not brought into the lounge or dining area. Telephone: 017466 762670.

- **HOW TO GET THERE:** Bridgnorth is located at the junction of the A442 and the A458.
- **PARKING:** For this walk it is advisable to use one of the long stay car parks. These are in Old Smithfield, at the rear of the Somerfield Supermarket, and at Innage Lane (the cheaper one on a Saturday) by the Fire Station, both are signposted.
- **LENGTH OF THE WALK:** 6½ miles. Map: OS Explorer 218 Wyre Forest & Kidderminster (GR 716932).

THE WALK

1. The starting point is the Town Hall in High Street, rebuilt in 1652 after a fire had destroyed most of the town. Go south down High Street and turn right into Listley Street passing the New Market Buildings on the left. Continue along Listley Street then turn left, down a ramp, into Railway Street, just prior to the Library and Tourist Information Centre. At the bottom of the steep and attractive Railway Street, cross the main road into Station Lane then follow it as it goes left. At the end, by the Severn Valley Railway repair shed turn right up a narrow path (not the tarmac track to the SVR car park).

2. Follow the path, uphill, to a school playing field, then cross it to walk alongside the tennis courts (it is a right of way). Cross a stile to a gravel track, then another back into the field and another to reach the Bridgnorth Bypass. Cross the footbridge and turn left onto a stony path, then after 50 yards cross a stile on the right to enter a field. Follow the right hedge (ignore a stile part way), then cross a stile in the field corner. Now go part left over the church parking area to reach the B4363 by Oldbury's church of St Nicholas. Turn left along the B4363 for 50 yards, turn right into the Old Mill Lane, then follow it to a road/track junction. Here turn right, now on a gravel track and, as that turns left, cross a stile to enter a field.

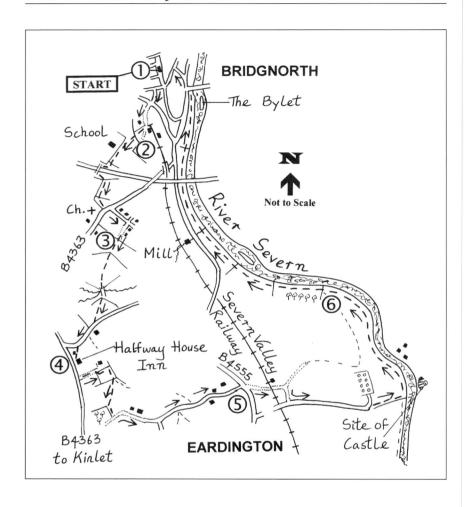

3. Proceed ahead, following a line of trees on the right, cross another stile and go over an open field, keeping to the right of an electricity pole near the middle of the field. Once past it keep the same direction and eventually a stile will become visible in the tree line ahead. Cross this to reach the footbridge at Potseething Spring. In the next field go part right towards a group of trees beyond the far hedge. At the hedge cross two stiles to a lane, turn right and follow it for about 200 yards (ignore a stile on the left). Just prior to reaching the B4363 take a drive off to the left, pass a house on the right, and go through a gate to the Halfway House Inn.

4. On leaving the inn turn left along the B4363 for 100 yards, then turn left along a drive (it is a bridlepath). On nearing a barn, and prior to the gateway ahead, cross a stile on the right by a gate. Follow the left hedge as it goes around the field to the far left corner and cross two stiles, then proceed directly across the next field to the corner of a wood. Here bear left, keeping the wood to your right, to a stile in the far right corner. Cross onto an unmade track and turn left, following the track as it turns right, passing farm buildings on the left, and goes gently downhill becoming a tarmac lane. Follow the lane to the village of Eardington and the B4555.

5. Cross the B4555 and almost immediately turn left to follow a gravel track to a level crossing over the Severn Valley Railway. Continue over to join a grassy track, turn right at a junction then turn left on reaching a tarmac road. Follow the tarmac lane downhill, enjoying the view. Enter woodland then, as the road turns left, keep ahead following the right edge of the field. Continue towards the Severn, a large sandstone outcrop being prominent ahead. It was on top of this outcrop that Roger de Montgomery constructed a motte and bailey castle. On reaching the river turn left to follow the riverside path upstream, now on the Severn Way. The path eventually leaves the large field at a stile, with high ground to the left.

6. The route now proceeds through trees, over pasture land, then on a narrow section above the river. Continue along the riverside path, under the bypass bridge, and eventually reach the now renovated Quayside by Bridgnorth Bridge. Across from the Quayside is The Bylet, formed by the construction of a barge gutter between it and the opposite bank to allow the passing of trows. To finish the walk cross the road and go up the Cartway, the original route from the Quayside up to High Town, full of interesting old dwellings, many of which used to be inns. As an alternative there are also the Cliff Railway or Stoneway Steps, both accessed from directly opposite the Quayside.

PLACES OF INTEREST NEARBY
Outside the town is *Daniel's Mill* at Eardington, a working water mill, open afternoons on Wednesday, Saturday, Sunday and Bank Holiday Monday from Easter to September. Telephone: 01746 762753.

WALK 15

HAMPTON LOADE AND CHELMARSH RESERVOIR

A walk with panoramic views that encompasses an ancient ford over the River Severn, Chelmarsh Reservoir, an old 'green lane', and the Mor Brook.

The River Severn near Chelmarsh

The starting point for this walk is the ferry over the Severn between the hamlets of Hampton, on the west bank, and Hampton Loade, on the east bank, originating because this was the site of an important ford across the river. The old passenger ferry here, powered by the flow of the river, is still in use. One of the more prominent features of the area, especially when viewed from the A442 Bridgnorth to Kidderminster Road, is Chelmarsh Reservoir, built to supply drinking water from water taken from the Severn.

Situated on the B4555 at Chelmarsh is the Bull's Head Inn, a fine old hostelry that also offers accommodation. As it is not situated on

70

a 'through' route it has to attract customers by good food and service and the range of dishes, from grills to Jambalaya, smoked haddock, grilled salmon, (my own choice), or Gloucester sausage, reflect this. Being a free house there is usually a good range of beers, including local ones such as 'Shropshire Lad', and also cider and lager. Food is available from 12 noon to 2 pm and 6.30 pm to 9.30 pm, all week. Telephone: 01746 861469.

- **HOW TO GET THERE:** Most people will probably reach the starting point from the A442 Bewdley to Kidderminster Road; just turn off at the junction signposted Hampton Loade. This will, however, mean using the ferry which only runs from April to September. (For information regarding the ferry operation the ferryman can be contacted via his mobile phone on 0966 183728.) Alternative parking places on the west bank, without using the ferry, are accessed from the B4555 Bridgnorth to Highley road, the Bull's Head Inn is on the B4555 and there is limited parking near the ferry, follow the narrow lane signposted Hampton Loade.
- **PARKING:** If starting from the east bank of the river there is a National Trust car park (chargeable to non members) by the river (GR 748865). On the west bank of the river there is limited parking (up to five cars) at the end of the lane beyond the SVR railway station (GR 747865). People intending to use the Bull's Head Inn can use the car park there (GR 722875), and start the walk from Point 4 in the route notes, however please contact the owner first (telephone: 01746 861469).
- **LENGTH OF THE WALK:** 6 miles. Map: OS Explorer 218 Wyre Forest & Kidderminster.

THE WALK

1. Having reached the west bank of the river there are two possibilities to start the walk. Those people interested in steam trains, and who want to visit the Hampton Loade station of the Severn Valley Railway, walk downstream and follow the lane to the station. On leaving the station turn left, and again follow the lane as it goes uphill and turns right. At the point where it turns left keep straight ahead to a stile on the right. This is Point 2; continue the walk from there (please see the map). Ramblers who prefer field paths walk upstream, river to the right, to cross a stile. Go 30 yards beyond the stile, turn left, and walk towards the Unicorn Inn. Go to

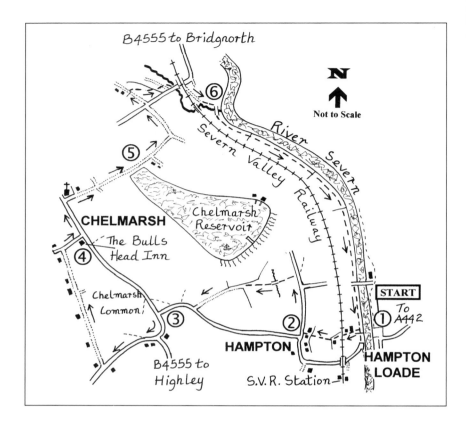

the left of the inn to the top right of the car parking area, go right, up a ramp, and almost immediately go left up some steps. Now carefully cross the Severn Valley Railway. Do watch out for the trains. Go up a path and through a gate marked 'Private Land' (it is a right of way). Keep to the right side of the garden and cross a stile to an arable field. Go straight up the field and soon a large group of farm buildings will become visible. Aim to the left of the large barn on the right and eventually cross a stile in the fence, by a large gate. Go through a farm machinery 'graveyard', bungalow and fence to the left, then use a stile, or gate if open, to a lane. Here turn right.

2. Follow the lane with views, right, over the Severn Valley. This lane is part of the Jack Mytton Way and goes to Chelmarsh Reservoir. It is followed to a point some 150 yards beyond the

Ferry between Hampton and Hampton Loade

'Private Road' going down to the pipe bridge; then go through the large metal gate on the left. (There is also a similar gate on the right.) Once through proceed straight across the field to a gate and culvert bridge in the far hedge, then go slightly right to join, and follow, a hedge of trees. At the top right corner of the field join an enclosed track but take time to look right to view Chelmarsh Reservoir, the dam, and the array of boats. Continue along the track to a lane, turn right to reach the B4555, then turn left.

3. Follow the road as it turns right past the King's Arms (well, perhaps there is time for a quick one!), but please use the verge for safety. As the road goes left keep straight ahead on a lane, signposted Billingsley, and follow this to a point just past an isolated house on the left. Immediately past the house, turn right onto a wide stony track (by The Denn Farm) and follow the track through Chelmarsh Common. At one time coal, sited near the surface, was mined here. The track now varies between stones, tarmac, gravel and grass as it passes farms and houses to reach a road at a T junction. Here turn right and follow the road to the B4555 and the Bull's Head Inn.

4. From the inn turn left along the B4555 and follow it to a point just before reaching St Peter's church. Here turn right and follow a tarmac drive, now on a bridlepath. Continue along the tarmac drive and, as it turns left, keep straight ahead on an unmade track. This deep sided track, an old 'green lane', goes downhill to a path junction. There keep ahead (now back on the Jack Mytton Way) and eventually emerge at the northern end of the Chelmarsh Reservoir.

5. Continue past the reservoir, a haven for wild life at this end, pass a house on the right and proceed along a tarmac drive (now leaving the Jack Mytton Way). Carry on until the drive turns left (ignore the wide track going right) and then meets the B4555. Take the track directly across the road. Follow the track to cross a stile by a gate, then turn right and cross another stile by a gate (if this stile is overgrown, use the gate). Now go down the arable field to a stile some 40 yards to the left of the end of the field. Turn right after the stile, cross a drive (to Astbury Hall, note the ornate iron gates) and then follow the Mor Brook on the left. Continue to the B4555, turn left, cross the Mor Brook and then go under the railway bridge. Take care because of the traffic. Once past the rail bridge turn right onto a gravel track, through a fishermen's car park, rejoin the Mor Brook and follow it to where it joins the River Severn.

6. Now it is a case of enjoying a waterside walk alongside the River Severn back to the start point. The route first goes over a cast iron bridge over the Mor Brook. This is a 19th century towpath bridge, to allow boats to be hauled up the Severn. This pleasant route first goes through trees, then pasture land, and has a good view of trains on the Severn Valley Railway. The path goes over another towpath bridge, under the pipe bridge (the building on the opposite bank being the pumping station), and eventually through a camping field and back to the ferry.

PLACES OF INTEREST NEARBY

Off the A442 is the National Trust property of *Dudmaston Hall*. This late 17th century house, with its paintings and sculptures, also has extensive gardens and woodland, with a number of large pools to provide even more 'waterside walks'. It is usually open during the afternoon, on Wednesday, Sunday and Bank Holiday Monday, from April to September. Telephone: 01746 780866.

HIGHLEY FROM THE SEVERN VALLEY COUNTRY PARK

A scenic and interesting walk combining the River Severn with the smaller Borle Brook, offering a contrast in landscape in an area where a Country Park has been created out of an industrial past.

The Ship Inn at Stanley

Highley is unusual in Shropshire in that part of it has the look of a northern industrial town, with its rows of terraced housing. This tends to hide the fact that Highley has a long history, having a Saxon based name and being recorded in the Domesday Book. It was, however, the natural resources of the area that caused Highley to be developed. Mining ceased in the late 1960s, the old pit and coal grading areas now being part of the Severn Valley Country Park. Flowing to the south of the village is the Borle Brook, which originates to the west of Bridgnorth then continues southwards to join the River Severn at Brooksmouth.

Not actually on the route but near the lane that leads from Alveley to the Country Park is the Three Horseshoes Inn. Dating from 1401 it claims to be 'the oldest pub in Shropshire' and has an evening restaurant. The lunch menu includes such dishes as chargrilled chicken (very good), rump steak, pork loin, also baked potatoes and sandwiches. The beer is Banks's, the ciders are Scrumpy Jack and Strongbow and the lagers are Harp and Fosters. Meals are available from 12 noon to 2.30 pm and 6.30 pm to 9 pm, Tuesday to Sunday. Telephone: 01746 780642. For those ramblers only wanting a 'bar snack' (breaded plaice, omelettes, etc), the Ship Inn is on the route (Point 2) by the riverside at the hamlet of Stanley. Food is generally available from 12 noon to 1.30 pm and 7 pm to 8.30 pm, all week. The beers are Worthington and Brew 11. Telephone: 01746 861219.

- **HOW TO GET THERE:** The Severn Valley Country Park is situated between the River Severn and Alveley. Access is through the village of Alveley from the A442. Follow the signs to the Country Park.
- **PARKING:** Ample free car parking at the Country Park.
- **LENGTH OF THE WALK:** 5 miles. Map: OS Explorer 218 Wyre Forest and Kidderminster (GR 754840).

THE WALK

1. From the visitor centre take the path in front of the windows and follow it downhill to the Colliery Bridge over the River Severn. Cross the bridge and immediately turn left, down the steps, to join the riverside path, the Severn Way. In parts the path here can be muddy but is passable by a combination of concrete slats or minor diversions. Soon the walk passes between the river and Highley Golf Course. After just over 1/2 mile the route enters Stanley, a small community that originated because of mining, sandstone quarries and the river trade. Today the cottages are let for holidays and it is the location for Highley Station on the Severn Valley Railway (the station is reached by the path up the side of the inn). There was once a passenger ferry across the river here. The wire support is still in position, across the river, by the first group of cottages reached.

2. Continue following the river downstream, now on a gravel/tarmac road. Then, as the road sweeps right, turn left down a drive and soon cross a stile to the left of a gate. Pass a large sandstone and brick house on the right and continue downstream, through a large

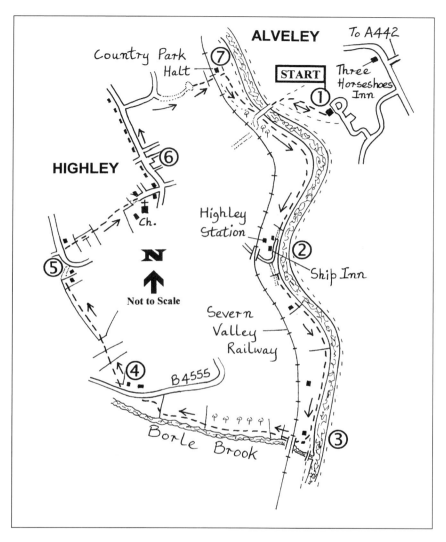

open field. Some 200 years ago the area to the right was also quarried for sandstone and mined for coal. Continue past two more houses, and over two more stiles, and immediately after the second house bear right, going between the houses and a ruined cottage. Before doing this it is worth going downstream for 100 yards to visit the cast iron Brooksmouth Bridge, cast at Ironbridge by the Coalbrookdale Company, in 1828.

Highley church and house

3. To continue with the walk, sweep around the house (on the right), then go left and right to pass under the Severn Valley Railway, the Borle Brook now on the left. The route now generally follows the brook, crossing a number of stiles, first going through a meadow and then through a wood. The path here can be quite muddy and care is necessary, particularly near the brook. In the wood the trees show extensive coppicing, probably for pit props for the mines. Leave the wood, go through a large field, again generally following the line of the brook, then cross a stile into a smaller field. Now go part right and uphill (the way directly ahead is boggy), and at the top of the field turn left, ignoring a gate. Follow the right hedge to reach steps and a stile, on the right, to the road. Here turn left and follow the road, with care, for some 200 yards to a stile on the right, passing a house, also on the right.

4. Having crossed the stile go part left and uphill to a gate and then go slightly right to the highest point ahead. Here go through another gate and follow the left fence, the view all around showing how undulating is this area. The valley immediately to the left is the Borle Brook. Cross the stile ahead with a fence/hedge on the left and follow a line of trees on the right, now walking along an old 'green lane'; the hill ahead/left is Brown Clee Hill. Soon cross a stile to a farm area and then another to a gravel track, passing houses on the right. This is the area of Netherton, now part of Highley but many years ago, before the mid 1800s, a separate community. Continue to the road and turn left.

5. Follow the road for about 100 yards then turn right, over a stile, to follow an enclosed path to a field. Now follow the left hedge to another stile. Go across a field, part of an old hedge line to the right, and eventually cross a stile in the very far right corner. Follow the right side of the grassy area to a gravel road and continue to the entrance to the churchyard. Adjacent is the beautiful Church House, once the home of the parish priest, the area around the church being the original settlement of Highley. Continue to the main road and turn left (notice the old school of 1863 on the corner, now the church hall), continuing into High Street. Proceed to the car park and public toilets on the right.

6. Continue northwards along High Street, passing Coronation Street, the Bache Arms (liquid refreshment but no food) and the Highley Welfare and Social Club, then turn right into Vicarage Lane. Proceed down the lane which soon becomes roughly surfaced and, as the lane sweeps left, keep to the track that goes right and over a cattle grid. Follow the enclosed track downhill, through a gate, and eventually reach a car turning area. Take the path to the right and reach the Country Park Halt of the Severn Valley Railway. Here carefully cross the rail track.

7. This area was once the coal grading plant and sidings for the coal mined at Alveley. All traces of past industrial use have now gone and the area transformed into a Country Park with a 'request' train stop. Having crossed the line join a wide track, turn right, and follow the track down to the bridge. Finally cross the bridge and return to the Visitor Centre.

PLACES OF INTEREST NEARBY
Just off the B4363, near Highley, is *Rays Farm Country Matters* with its collection of unusual farm animals, birds, tea room and gift shop. Telephone: 01299 841255.

UPPER ARLEY AND
THE RIVER SEVERN

Following the banks of the River Severn for the entire route, the walk encompasses coppice woodland, an old ferry crossing and a 16th century inn, with the opportunity to visit two Severn Valley Railway stations (and cheat by having a train ride upstream!).

The old ferry crossing at Upper Arley

Anyone travelling along the A442, Bridgnorth to Kidderminster section, passes through the eastern edge of Alveley and sees a modern village. However, hidden away at the western side is the old settlement that goes back to Saxon times and was listed in the Domesday Book. Today the village has a significant amenity for the rambler in the form of the Severn Valley Country Park, which in itself has an interesting, if somewhat more modern, history. During the 19th century coal was being mined in the Highley and Billingsley areas, but by the 1930s new shafts had been sunk at

Alveley and the main activity moved to there, resulting in the Colliery Bridge being built in 1936. The mine was, however, closed during 1968/69, the site becoming a derelict wasteland. In 1988 the Bridgnorth District Council and Shropshire County Council, with the aid of various grants, including one from the EEC, transformed the area into the Severn Valley Country Park. This is truly a tremendous transformation, from a grey wasteland to a 'green' environment full of wildlife.

At Upper Arley and on the route is the Harbour Inn, reputedly 16th century and built to serve the river and ferry trade, the name originating from the transfer of goods between river and land here, thus avoiding taxes and handling charges at Bewdley. It still caters for the traveller with a range of meals and bar snacks that include gammon steaks, large Yorkshire Puddings, hot mackerel and tummy filling steak sandwiches. The main beers are Banks and Boddingtons with the usual range of lagers and cider. Food is available from 12 noon to 2 pm and 7 pm to 9 pm, all week. Telephone: 01299 401204.

- **HOW TO GET THERE:** The Severn Valley Country Park is situated between the River Severn and Alveley. Access is through the village of Alveley from the A442 Bridgnorth to Kidderminster road. Follow the signs to the Country Park.
- **PARKING:** Ample free parking at the Country Park.
- **LENGTH OF THE WALK:** 6 miles. Map: OS Explorer 218 Wyre Forest and Kidderminster (GR 754840).

THE WALK

1. From the visitor centre take one of the paths going downhill towards the River Severn. It seems hard to imagine now that this slope was once a large grey spoil heap from the mine workings. On reaching the river turn left and follow the riverside path. In the summer this will be lined with Himalayan Balsam and dragon and damsel flies will be much in evidence. The path continues downstream entering coppice woodland, coppicing being the practice of cutting down trees at the base and allowing smaller stems to grow. The resulting thinner, and straight, stems could be used for a variety of purposes, in this case probably pit-props for the mines. Just prior to leaving the wood notice the large mill stone blank on the ground, to the right of the path – the reason for it

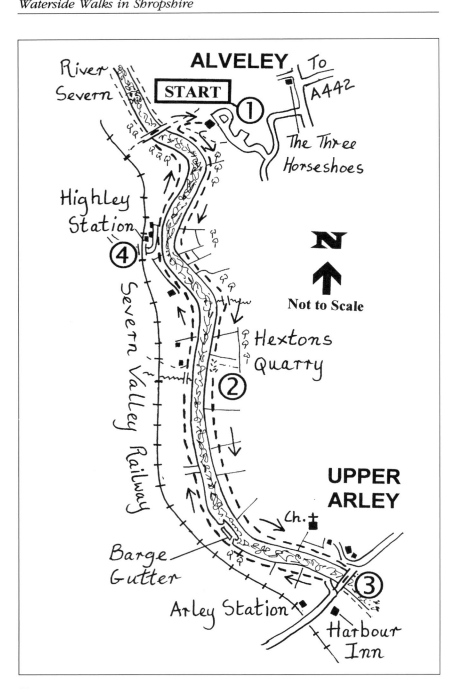

Severn Valley Country Park and Visitor Centre

being here is a mystery. Continue past the Ship Inn on the opposite bank, going downstream to eventually cross a footbridge; the Shropshire/Worcestershire boundary. Proceed downstream to reach cut sandstone blocks discarded by the riverside. A considerable amount of sandstone was quarried at Hexton's Quarry nearby and transported by river for building purposes.

2. Continue downstream to eventually reach the village of Upper Arley. If time permits it is worth doing a little exploring, the parish church of St Peter has Norman origins with later additions and an 18th century tower. Another point of interest is the site of the old ferry crossing. A ferry was recorded here as early as 1323 and the last ferry was used until 1972, when it was superseded by the present iron bridge. Having explored Upper Arley to the full, cross over the bridge for the return journey upstream, or to the Harbour Inn for refreshments.

3. The return route is now upstream on the west bank. However, for steam train enthusiasts a visit to Arley Station is worthwhile. (Also, for those who want to cheat a little, it is possible to catch the

Bridgnorth train to Highley Station and resume the walk from Point 4.) Arley Station has been featured in a number of film and TV productions, one of the latter being *Oh, Dr Beeching*. Now to continue with the walk, follow the riverside path northwards, passing the old ferry landing point, going through a kissing gate, and enjoying the view across to Upper Arley. The path is now on the Severn Way, identified by the Severn Trow symbol. Negotiate a muddy section of path then, at the third stile from the bridge, on emerging from the woods into a field, look out for a deep cutting on the right now overgrown with trees. This cutting was once a 'barge gutter'. In two places it has had causeways built across so sheep can now use the land on what had been an artificially created island, but the size of the 'gutter' or 'cut', can be viewed by going onto the middle causeway. Continue on the Severn Way, soon re-entering Shropshire, and passing over the Borle Brook. This old towpath bridge was cast by the Coalbrookdale Company at Ironbridge, the same company that made the Iron Bridge. Continue past the site of the sandstone blocks on the opposite bank, pass some houses, a fence on the left, then cross a stile to a road. Soon turn sharp right, to follow the road to the Ship Inn.

4. Continue upstream past the Ship Inn and, by the second group of cottages, look for a wire across the river from a pole to a tree on the opposite bank. This was the site of an old passenger ferry that could take anglers and visitors across the river. Once past the cottages keep to the riverside path (fence left, river right) and soon the route is alongside Highley Golf Course. Eventually the Colliery Bridge comes into view and the path meanders through woodland but generally follows the line of the river. It can be very muddy here but there are a number of concrete walkways and path variations to avoid the worse parts. At the bridge go up the steps, cross it, then follow one of the paths that go uphill to the visitor centre.

PLACES OF INTEREST NEARBY
Some 7 miles to the south is the riverside town of Bewdley with the *West Midlands Safari Park* and the *Severn Valley Railway*. The local Tourist Information Centre has full details. Telephone: 01299 404740.

THE RIVER REA AT
CLEOBURY MORTIMER

*A short walk through the small, but very interesting, old town of
Cleobury Mortimer, prior to joining the meandering River Rea. There
are views, northwards, over south Shropshire, and to the south and
east over north Worcestershire.*

The ford over the river at Neen Savage

Cleobury Mortimer is a small town dating back to before the
Norman invasion, after which it was given to Ralph de Mortimer
who made it his main residence, thus adding his name to the town.
Eventually the family moved to the more secure and substantial
castle at Ludlow, so Cleobury Castle, believed to have been situated
behind the church, is no more. St Mary's church, which dates from
the latter part of the 12th century, is famed for its crooked spire. The
twist is due to the natural warping of its wooden frame, and even
the tiles that cover it (some 80,000 in total) are made of wood. To

the east of the town is the River Rea, which starts life to the north of Brown Clee Hill as the Rea Brook, then meanders south to join the River Teme just inside Worcestershire. The old name for the river was 'Neen', hence such places as Neen Savage and Neen Sollars on its course. As a 'working' river it had numerous mills (fulling, wood turning, paper making, etc).

Within the town there are many good hostelries and on this occasion, I enjoyed a meal at the Royal Fountain Inn, situated in the main street opposite the church and close to the old town well. There is always a range of home made 'specials' available at lunch time (my spinach and broccoli lasagne would have kept Popeye happy), which usually include a daily 'roast' and also hot and cold snacks. There is a full 'a la carte' menu of an evening. It is an old timber framed building, possibly 17th century, brick clad at the front but with a wealth of beams inside, and there is also a patio garden at the rear, complete with a fountain. Being a free house there is a range of real ales, cider, lager and wines, etc with meals available from 12.30 pm to 2 pm all week, and 7.30 pm to 9 pm Tuesday to Saturday. Telephone: 01299 270177.

- **HOW TO GET THERE:** Cleobury Mortimer is on the A4117 between Bewdley and Ludlow.
- **PARKING:** A free public car park is situated behind the Talbot Hotel, access is from Childe Road (see route map).
- **LENGTH OF THE WALK:** 3 or 4^1/$_2$ miles. Map: OS Explorer 218 Wyre Forest & Kidderminster or Explorer 203 Ludlow, Tenbury Wells & Cleobury Mortimer (GR 673758).

THE WALK

1. From the car park entrance turn right into Childe Road and after 100 yards go left onto an enclosed path (by Ronville). Continue ahead at a road, and then over crossroads. Pass a school on the left, then cross a stile. Continue into the field, now with views over south Shropshire, Titterstone Clee Hill to the left. Bear slightly right to join a fence and follow it downhill (steep in parts) to a stile and then a footbridge over a brook, the parish boundary.

2. Follow the path that goes right and gently uphill (brook on the right) to reach a farm. Cross the stile ahead, to the left of the drive, turn left and follow the left hedge. Cross a stile to a tarmac lane then

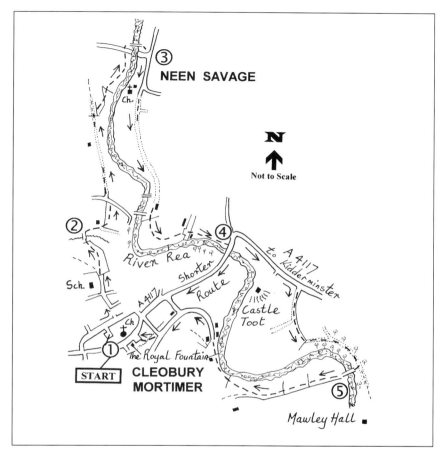

go straight ahead on a partly surfaced bridleway, 'Musbatch Farm —
Private Drive'. Pass the farm (left), continue on an enclosed path, go
through a gate and then cross a stile on the right. Go downhill
through the trees and enter a meadow. Follow the left fence, go
through a gate and bear slightly right, the River Rea over to the
right. Cross a stile to a lane, then turn right and reach a footbridge
and ford over the Rea. At times of low water in the river it can be
tempting to walk across the ford, however it can be very slippery.

3. Once over the Rea turn right, passing Neen Savage church on the
right. Continue along the road and, as it sweeps left, take the
unmade track on the right, ignoring a drive and gates off it. Soon it

becomes a dirt track, then passes a pipe bridge over the Rea, the Elan Valley pipeline supplying water to Birmingham. Also, near this spot was a paper mill, now only the weir over the river remains. On reaching a house (Walfords Bridge), cross the stile ahead, and follow the river as it sweeps left. At a weir, where the river bends and shown by the line of a hollow in the field, is the site of an old mill race to what was another paper mill. Here the old workers' cottages remain, on the left after going through the kissing gate. Not surprisingly they are called Paper Mill Cottages. Continue ahead via a kissing gate and then a stile, following the river to a road bridge. Go up steps to the road. Then, for the shorter walk, turn right and return to Cleobury. For the longer walk read on.

4. For the full walk cross the road, turn left and follow the sidewalk, going uphill, past Newbridge Nursery and a house drive. Some 150 yards past the drive take a wide dirt track on the right. Follow this, with views ahead over north Worcestershire and right towards Cleobury. Ahead/left is Mawley Hall. On the right the mound with the house is the strangely named Castle Toot, thought to be an Iron Age hill fort. Where the track goes right continue ahead, following the left fence. Go through a bridlegate and follow a wide, grassy track that goes closer to the River Rea down on the right. Look for a footbridge over the river and cross it. Just downstream from here is the site of a forge mill, where wrought iron was produced.

5. Now continue ahead alongside the left fence, crossing two stiles. Below, right, is the Rea with Brown Clee Hill on the horizon. On approaching a gate in the fence, a farm ahead, go part right and downhill, towards Cleobury. Cross a stile, pass a cottage on the left, then another stile to a tarmac lane, the site of yet another mill. Follow the lane, then take the road passing to the left of the Medical Centre. Turn right at the next lane. After 20 yards turn left onto a narrow path, Pudding Brook on the right. Follow the path to reach the old town well, then turn left at the main road for the Royal Fountain Inn and then the car park at the rear of the Talbot Hotel.

PLACES OF INTEREST NEARBY
Some 5 miles south of Cleobury, on the A456 Bewdley to Tenbury Wells road, is the *Mamble Craft Centre*, created from an old barn and complete with a craft gallery, gift shop, tea room and workshops.

WALK 19
BROMFIELD AND THE RIVER TEME

A delightful walk from the historic village of Bromfield, crossing the River Onny, following a short section of the River Teme, then taking field paths with superb panoramic views across southern Shropshire.

The River Teme at Bromfield

Bromfield is almost entirely owned by the Earl of Plymouth, who also owns Oakley Park, which is administered from the Estate Offices in the village. Bromfield was mentioned in the Domesday Book as having a collegiate church, that became part of the Benedictine Priory founded in the 12th century. All that remains of the priory now is the magnificent 14th century gatehouse, some ruins behind the parish church, and the church itself, St Mary's, noted for its painted chancel ceiling. The history of the area is also much older than the Norman remains indicate, as the area between The Cookhouse and the Race Course is the site of a Roman encampment.

The River Teme starts life in the Kerry Hill area south of Newtown in Wales, and runs through Shropshire to exit the county just south of Ludlow. By contrast, the River Onny is a Shropshire river, being formed by the River West Onny and the River East Onny joining to the west of the Long Mynd. The river then runs south through Craven Arms to join the Teme at Bromfield.

The Cookhouse at Bromfield has quite a history in itself. This old Georgian farmhouse was converted to an inn, the Clive Arms, named after Robert Clive of India. The premises have again been converted, now into a café, pub and restaurant, three separate options in one building, with food available from 9 am to 9 pm. Between them the three entities offer a very wide range of speciality teas, coffees, and real ale (Tetley and Hobsons). Food starts with a breakfast menu (my smoked salmon and scrambled egg breakfast made a good start to the walk), through to lunches (prawn & avocado salad, pork & spinach cannelloni, etc), to a full range of evening meals. There is also a selection of children's and vegetarian meals. Telephone: 015841 856565.

- **HOW TO GET THERE:** Bromfield is on the A49, 3 miles north west of Ludlow.
- **PARKING:** Ample parking to the front of The Cookhouse (the old A49).
- **LENGTH OF THE WALK:** 5 miles. Map: OS Explorer 203 Ludlow, Tenbury Wells & Cleobury Mortimer (GR 483770).

THE WALK

1. From The Cookhouse go north along the A49. Cross the bridge over the River Onny, then cross the road (the pedestrian underpass is the safest route). Now take the first turning left to pass the church of St Mary the Virgin and the imposing gatehouse of the dissolved Benedictine priory. Continue along the 'Private Road' (it is a right of way, a bridlepath) and just before the bridge over the Teme cross a stile on the right, taking care on the big step down. Now follow the river bank, soon crossing a stile to the left of a gate to follow the path between the river, left, and a field fence, right. Care is needed here as this path can be uneven and possibly overgrown, but it is used. This is where a stout 'nettle whacker' can be put to good use. Follow the path until a gate is visible ahead, then look for a stile on the right, before reaching the gate. Cross the stile, go up the bank, then follow the left field edge to reach a track that enters a field on

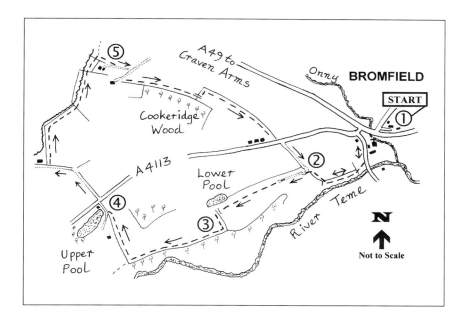

the left. The field you have just walked up is called 'Crawl Meadow'. A local legend tells the story of a young maid, from Bromfield, whose marriage gift was to be as much land as she could crawl over in one day. This meadow is that portion of land.

2. Go through the gate into a large field, and follow a wide track as it turns right and then left to run parallel to the hedge over to the right. The official footpath line as shown on maps is alongside the hedge, however that line is not used, and the stiles at the far end of the field are in line with the track. Follow the track for the full length of the field, passing some electricity poles and then trees, with a pool beyond (Lower Pool) over to the right. On this section the tree-covered hill to the left is High Vinnalls. At the far end of the field cross two stiles close together, turn left, then follow the left hedge.

3. At the top corner of the field turn right and continue following the field edge, fence and wood (Stocking Nursery) to the left. Now a different view unfolds as the route progresses along the top of the field. Ahead the view is towards the Leintwardine area, and nearing the end of the field, the view right is towards Craven Arms with the southern end of the Long Mynd visible in the distance. Continue to the far corner of the field and again turn right. Continue along the field edge (farm over to the left), and near the far end of the field go through a gate and turn right along a track. Pass over the dam of Upper Pool, a fishing pool, to reach the A4113.

4. Cross the road and take the wide stony track opposite, a bridlepath, with panoramic views all around. Follow the track as it sweeps left then, on approaching Cookeridge Cottages, cross a stile on the right. Again follow the left side of the field, fence and trees to the left. There is also a small brook beyond the fence, not visible until later, which is the county boundary between Herefordshire and Shropshire. Continue along the field edge as it sweeps right and follow it until it sweeps right again, here look for a stile in the hedge on the left. (Look carefully, it might be overgrown.) Once over the stile follow the line of the brook, keeping to the right of it, and then cross a stile to an old orchard area, with a house over to the right. Go across the small area to a stile at the far side, cross and negotiate about 5 yards of undergrowth (time to use the 'nettle whacker' again). In the next field turn right. Go up the field to join the concrete drive to the house.

5. Now follow the drive away from the house. Continue to the end of the drive and at a T junction turn right, again on a concrete drive. On approaching a house turn left and now follow the right edge of the field, soon passing Cookeridge Wood on the right. At the far corner of the field cross a footbridge and immediately turn left, now following the left edge of the field which soon turns right. Follow this field edge to eventually meet the A4113. Go left for some 20 yards, then cross the road and follow a wide track, ditch to the right. Keep on the track for about 300 yards to where it turns right, into a field. This is Point 2 on the route map. Retrace your steps back along the River Teme to the start.

PLACES OF INTEREST NEARBY

As it is only 3 miles away, this has to be *Ludlow*, with its castle, museum, shops, narrow streets, great church and numerous old and interesting buildings. The best suggestion is to visit the Tourist Information Centre in Castle Street, buy a Town Trail, and explore. Telephone: 01584 875053.

BISHOP'S CASTLE AND THE INFANT RIVER KEMP

Bishop's Castle has a wealth of historic buildings, the Shropshire Way runs through it and the infant River Kemp rises to the west of the town. Add to this superb scenery and a nearby Iron Age hill fort, and this walk provides a wonderful day out.

The infant River Kemp

Bishop's Castle takes its name from a castle built by Robert Losinga, Bishop of Hereford 1079-1095 but as the location was not of major strategic importance, the castle fell into disrepair and was 'finished off' by the Civil War. The town however prospered as a market town and still has the original Norman layout. Down the centre of the town, through High Street and Church Street, runs the Shropshire Way, a circular route of some 140 miles. A section of the Shropshire Way, to the south-west of Bishop's Castle, runs beside a small stream, unnamed on OS maps but which the local inhabitants say is the infant River Kemp. This pastoral stream rises to the south of Bishop's Moat, runs through the Colebatch Valley (the location of this walk) and eventually flows to join the River Clun by Aston-on-Clun.

At the top of the town in the Market Square, not on the route of the walk but passed if using the Town Trail, is The Poppy House. This large 17th century (and possibly much older) dwelling is a combination of tea room, restaurant and guest house, serving superb home made cakes, soups and interesting lunches (mainly vegetarian but with some meat dishes). There is also a good wine list and a range of bottled beers from the local Three Tuns Brewery. It is open from 10 am to 5 pm all week so is ideal to start or finish the walk. Telephone: 01588 638443. At the bottom of the town, and passed twice on the walk, is the Six Bells Inn and Brewery. The inn was first licensed in 1750, the old brewery was re-established in 1997 and now brews a range of real ale, including the award winning 'Cloud Nine'. Food is served 12 noon to 2 pm Thursday to Sunday, and also on Friday and Saturday evenings, and includes such dishes as lamb, rum & prune casserole. The inn is closed on Monday lunch time. So, between the two premises there is ample fare to satisfy even the most hungry of walkers (but take care, too many pints of 'Cloud Nine' and you might not even start the walk!). Telephone: 01588 630144.

- **HOW TO GET THERE:** Bishop's Castle is just off the A488, about 2 miles south of its junction with the A489.
- **PARKING:** The main car park (free) is in Harley Jenkins Street, which is off High Street, opposite the post office. Also (when not in use) the Auction Market in Station Street.
- **LENGTH OF THE WALK:** $3^1/_2$ miles. Map: OS Explorer 216 Welshpool & Montgomery (GR 323888).

THE WALK

1. The walk starts from the post office, which is almost opposite the end of Harley Jenkins Street and near the point where High Street, (which goes north) and Church Street (which goes south) merge. Proceed down Church Street, passing the King's Head and the Boar's Head Hotel, to arrive at the Six Bells Inn and Brewery. Cross the road towards the church (St John the Baptist), turn right and almost immediately left into Church Lane.

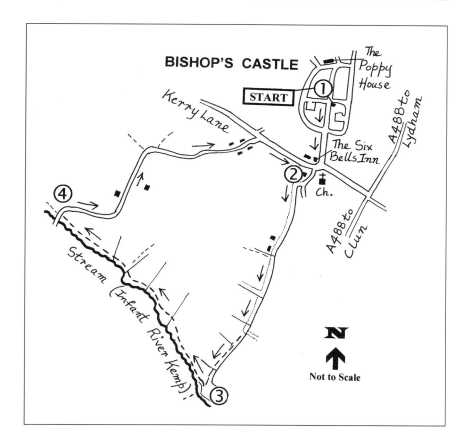

2. Proceed along Church Lane, past the Fire Station, and just over 100 yards from the beginning of the lane turn right onto a dirt track, signposted 'Field Lane'. After about 30 yards turn left and then follow the enclosed track as it goes gently uphill. The route here, and indeed from its start in Church Street, is on the Shropshire Way. As the track ends at some houses go through the large gate directly ahead, pass a house on the right, then cross a stile to a grassy track. At this point there is a sweeping view, to the left, across south Shropshire. Soon the track is enclosed again and then proceeds through a gate (ignore the track going right), becoming stony. The view ahead now opens up. Initially keep on the track to a stile, then go directly ahead, ignoring the track as it goes left, and continuing along the left edge of the field. Soon after crossing the next stile leave the hedge to go straight down the open field. On approaching a stile at the bottom do not cross it but turn right to follow a stream now on your left.

3. The route now generally follows the stream, the infant River Kemp. This beautiful little stream takes on a variety of guises on its meandering course as it is followed for just over a mile. Sometimes deep, sometimes wide and shallow, through trees, then meadows, over stones, almost lost in high grass, it is constantly changing, yet always flowing to eventually find its way to the Severn and the sea. The route crosses four stiles and then enters a small lane via a gate. Here turn right.

4. The route back now follows the lane, possibly dirt covered at first, as it goes uphill, sweeps left and then right, and after about 1 mile reaches the outskirts of Bishop's Castle. On the way back there are occasional views towards the eastern side of the Long Mynd. Eventually reach some houses then, at a road junction, turn right, following the road to reach the Six Bells Inn and Brewery. From here on you are 'on your own' for a wander around Bishop's Castle. Unless, of course, it's your turn to buy a round!

PLACES OF INTEREST NEARBY
Some 4 miles south of the town, accessed from a country lane that runs from the B4385 at Brockton to the B4368 at Clunton, is the *Bury Ditches Iron Age hill fort*. It is located on the top of Sunnyhill (Forest Enterprise land) and is signposted from both directions, there are also a number of marked Nature Trails. From the car park a gentle 1 mile walk to the top and back is amply rewarded with a superb 360° panoramic view over south-west Shropshire.